Seafood Cooking for Your Health

Seafood Cooking for Your Health

By Shizuko Yoshida

Japan Publications, Inc.

Published by JAPAN PUBLICATIONS, INC., Tokyo and New York

Distributors:
UNITED STATES: *Kodansha International/USA, Ltd., through Farrar, Straus & Giroux, 19 Union Square West, New York, 10003.* CANADA: *Fitzhenry & Whiteside Ltd., 195 Allstate Parkway, Markham, Ontario, L3R 4T8.* BRITISH ISLES: *Premier Book Marketing Ltd., 1 Gower Street, London WC1E 6HA.* EUROPEAN CONTINENT: *European Book Service PBD, Strijkviertel 63, 3454 PK De Meern, The Netherlands.* AUSTRALIA AND NEW ZEALAND: *Bookwise International, 54 Crittenden Road, Findon, South Australia 5007.* THE FAR EAST AND JAPAN: *Japan Publications Trading Co., Ltd., 1–2–1, Sarugaku-cho, Chiyoda-ku, Tokyo 101.*

First edition: November 1989

LCCC No. 88–81758
ISBN 0–87040–783–x

Printed in U.S.A.

Foreword

Living in an island nation, the Japanese people are very fond of fish and other
kinds of seafood, of which they enjoy a great abundance. Their fondness reflects
in some slightly romantic tendencies, like the practice of referring to sea bream
as *sakura-dai*, or cherry bream, in the spring, when the cherry trees are in bloom
or like employing a character composed of one elment meaning fish and another
meaning snow for cod, which is most delicious in the severe winter.

But aside from fancies of this kind, together with *tofu* (bean curd), fish have long
been a major source of protein in the Japanese diet. The antiquity of the habit of
eating fish is witnessed by fish bones and sea shells found together with bones of
birds and other beasts in archaeological mounds associated with prehistoric
dwelling locations.

With the introduction of Buddhism in the sixth century, the eating of animal
flesh became taboo for religious reasons and remained generally unpopular until
the middle part of the nineteenth century. Consequently, during those centuries,
fish and tofu, prepared in a variety of ingenious ways, some distinctive to the local
cultures of given regions, were of supreme dietary importance.

I learned much about the flavors and varieties of foods from the sea as a child
while living on the shores of the Seto Inland Sea, a region noted for various local
seafood specialties. A long, narrow body of water with a temperate climate—not
unlike that of the Mediterranean—the Seto Inland Sea provides an abundance of
different kinds of seafoods the year round. One of the most exciting events of the
year is netting sea bream in early spring. The nets are spread out and pulled by
several boats to enclose the fish, which glitter pink in the sun when, finally, the
nets are pulled in. The fish are scaled and cleaned at once and then cooked together with rice on the boat. Fanned by cooling sea breezes, everyone is more than
ready to enjoy this famous dish, served right on the boat, when it is ready, usually
just at noontime.

I have spent two periods of my life in the United States. Beginning in 1970, I
lived with my family in New York for four years. And then, beginning in 1985,
I spent two years in Los Angeles. During the first of the two periods, supermarket
fish departments were relegated to distant corners; and what they had for sale
could hardly be described as of the freshest. When I wanted fish, I traveled to the
harbor to buy directly from fishermen or, once in every few months, visited one
of the few nearby fish stores. I enjoyed both kinds of excursion.

In Los Angeles in the eighties, however, things were very different. I was
delighted to see that fish departments in supermarkets were prominent, large, well-
lighted, and very clean. In addition, my family and I enjoyed going to seafood
markets at nearby beaches, where we found plenty of whole fish that we could

have roasted on the spot. Shrimps and crabs too were cooked there. And it was fun to relax and delight in the breezes and in delicious crab (we cracked their shells with wooden mallets).

Eating habits, which are deeply related to history and traditions, stubbornly resist change. Nonetheless there is always room for improvement, which is not all that difficult to achieve if the truth about eating is clearly understood.

It is sometimes said that human beings adopt one of three approaches to eating: to eat with the belly, the mouth, or the head. Eating with the belly means doing nothing but assuaging hunger pangs and is the lowest level. Eating with the mouth means eating things that taste good, without regard to their nutritional values. This is somewhat higher than the lowest level. Finally, eating with the head means choosing foods with an eye to the effect they have on health. Although your dietary tradition may not till now have included them, fish and other seafoods are good for you. Knowing this, why not use your head and begin now enjoying more nutritious seafoods. I feel certain you will like them if you try them.

Moreover, you will be fascinated to discover the many new and different ways in which seafoods can be prepared. Having studied cooking in the United States, I have attempted to share what I learned there with the women of Japan. At the same time, I am eager to carry the knowledge of Japanese seafood culture to the peoples of other countries. This is why I have written this book.

In conclusion, I should like to express my profound gratitude to my friend Reiko Kosugi for invaluable consultation and cooperation.

Reports on the latest information on nutritional aspects of seafoods are one of the most distinguishing characteristics of this book. In connection with this topic I am very grateful to Sachiko Okuda, Ph.D., director of the Fuji Television Merchandise Research Center and a specialist in the field, who was extremely generous in providing advice.

Iwao Yoshizaki, president of Japan Publications, Inc., assisted me by constantly keeping the main concept of the book clearly before me and by making available the most up-to-date information. Finally, I should like to express my gratitude to the translator Richard L. Gage, the designer Tatsundo Hayashi, the photographer Kazuo Sugiyama, the food stylist Kiyomi Sugiyama, the illustrator Eriko Satoh, and the editor Yotsuko Watanabe.

Shizuko Yoshida

Goals of This Book

In recent years it has become clear that excessive intake of calories and animal fats is intimately related to such diseases as cardiac infarction, angina pectoris, cerebral thrombosis, and so on, which account for a growing number of deaths in Japan as well as in Europe and America. This knowledge has stimulated many people to reexamine the importance of fish, which are low in calories and high in protein and the oil of which contains EPA (eicosapentaenoic acid) and DHA (docosahexaenoic acid), thought to be a preventative of cardiovascular disease. The taurin in squid, shrimps, and such shellfish as oysters is thought to have a similar preventative effect; and sea vegetables are believed to prevent certain kinds of cancer.

In the hope of stimulating more people in the West to eat and enjoy nutritious and valuable foods from the sea, in this book, I introduce one hundred and twenty-four recipes from the traditional Japanese repertory that are delicious and simple and quick to prepare in a Western kitchen. Though most of them require only ordinary ingredients, they are all good enough to serve to company. Quantities of oils and salt are kept to a minimum.

Ingredients unavailable in ordinary American supermarkets will be found on the shelves of stores specializing in oriental foods. My principal goal in writing this book is to stimulate you to try these wholesome, delicious recipes in your own kitchen and make them a lasting part of your dietary repertory.

Spring

(top to bottom) Scallops with Tofu Sauce (p. 17), Dried *Sakura* Shrimp and *Wakame* Pilaf (p. 108), Clam Broth (p. 42), Gold-roast Sea Bream (p. 88)

Summer

(top to bottom) Shrimp and Chicken Savory Custard (*Chawan-mushi*) (p. 46), *Jako* and *Daikon* Salad (p. 32), Broiled Salmon with Sesame and Ginger (p. 84), Scallop *Teriyaki* (p. 17), Yellowtail *Teriyaki* (p. 63)

Autumn

(top to bottom) Miso Soup with *Wakame* and Tofu (p. 45), Sea-delicacies Salad (p. 35), Mixed Tempura (p. 68) and Crab and *Wakame* Fritters (p. 80)

Winter

(top to bottom) Cod and Shrimp Casserole with Potatoes (p. 95), Salmon and Tofu Mini-croquettes (p. 19), Fancy-tied *Kamaboko* (p. 16), Confetti Sushi (p. 103), Fancy Cucumbers and Salmon Roe (p. 16), Salmon Rice (p. 105), Cod Paprika (p. 91)

Contents

Appetizers and Salads

Deep-fried Tofu
with Shrimp (p. 19)

Appetizers should stimulate not overwhelm the appetite. They should be in bite-size pieces. Made small, many of the main dishes presented in this book could serve as appetizing first courses.

Seafood appetizers are an elegant, light way to arouse pleasing expectations about the meal to come.

Shrimp Flowers

The shrimps are rounded and fried a delicate pink.

> $\frac{1}{2}$ lb shrimp
> $\frac{1}{3}$ tsp salt
> 1 Tbsp white wine
> Cornstarch
> Oil for frying
> Boston lettuce
> Lemon

1. Devein the shrimp. Shell, leaving the tail shell intact.
2. Cut and open flat. Sprinkle with salt and white wine and allow to stand for 20 minutes.
3. Dry each shrimp on paper towels. Using the tip of a knife, jiggle the tail shell

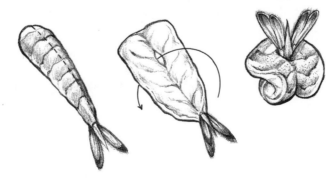

to make sure moisture underneath is eliminated. About 1/3 the way from the forward end of the shrimp, make a vertical slit about 1/3 in long.

4.   After inserting the tail through the slit made in step *3*, open the tail shell and spread it flat.

5.   Sprinkle with cornstarch.

6.   In a fairly deep frying pan, heat oil to 350°F and fry the shrimp for a minute or 2 for small to medium varieties. Be careful not to overcook. Drain on paper towels.

7.   Arrange Boston lettuce on a serving plate. Place shrimps on top and garnish with lemon wedges.

Fancy Cucumbers and Salmon Roe

This colorful and delicious, though simple, appetizer consists of miniature cucumber cups topped with caviar—red or black. The same method of cutting may be used with celery stalks.

> **2 Japanese-style cucumbers**
> **1 oz salmon roe or caviar**
> **Parsley**
> **Radishes**

1.   Wash cucumbers and cut them into 2-in lengths.

2.   Make incisions *a* and *b* in alphabetical order. Twist the cucumber in the direction of the arrow.

3.   With the tip of a spoon or a melon-scoop make a shallow depression in the center. Salt lightly and fill with salmon roe or caviar. Arrange on a serving dish together with a garnish of parsley and radishes. Adjust the quantities of salmon roe to suit your individual taste. Japanese-style cucumbers, which are smaller and more tender than Western ones, may be found in gourmet supermarkets.

Fancy-tied *Kamaboko*

Cut *kamaboko* 1/3 in thick in the shape shown in *1* or *2* for use as hors d'oeuvres.

When the *kamaboko* is mounded high, incisions can be made in it for fancy-tied forms. *A* is the underside and *B* the upper side.

Thick-sliced ham or sausage may be prepared in the same way.

Scallop *Teriyaki*

This aromatic hors d'oeuvre is simple to make. It employs frozen scallops marinated in soy sauce flavored with ginger and garlic and baked in an oven.

$\frac{2}{3}$ **lb scallops**
Leaf lettuce
Marinade:
    4 Tbsp soy sauce
    2 Tbsp sakè or sherry
    1 Tbsp sesame oil
    $\frac{1}{2}$ **tsp grated fresh ginger**
    $\frac{1}{2}$ **tsp crushed garlic**

1. Combine marinade ingredients and marinate scallops for 2 hours. If scallops are large, slice them horizontally in 2.
2. Preheat the oven to 400°F. Line a baking dish with baking paper or greased aluminum foil. Dry the scallops on paper towels and arrange them in the baking dish. Bake for 4 minutes. Turn the scallops once and bake another minute. Turn again and bake 1 minute longer.
3. Garnish a serving dish with leaf lettuce and arrange the scallops in the center.

Scallops with Tofu Sauce *(Serves 4)*

Popular because of their pleasing mildness, mixed dishes dressed with a tofu-based sauce flavored with sesame—called *shira-ae* in Japanese—can include any of a wide variety of ingredients.

    6 scallops
    3 dried *shiitake* mushrooms or champignons
    1 oz carrot
    ⅓ block *konnyaku* (devil's tongue jelly)
    Watercress
    1 Japanese-style cucumber
    Salt
  Sauce:
    ½ block cotton (*momen*) tofu
    2 Tbsp white sesame seeds or 1 tsp tahini
    1 tsp soy sauce
    1 tsp sakè
    1 tsp sugar
    ⅓ tsp salt

1.   Lightly toast sesame seeds and grind them in a mortar or food processor. Drain the tofu well beforehand (see p. 19). Add tofu to the contents of the mortar or food processor and mix well. Add the remaining sauce ingredients and blend thoroughly. (Soften tahini with liquid ingredients and seasoning before mixing it with tofu.)

2.   Wash scallops. Soften dried *shiitake* mushrooms in lukewarm water then simmer in broth (pp. 37–39) for 10 minutes. Drain well and slice thin. (Champignons may be sliced thin and parboiled.) Julienne cut carrot and parboil to crisp-tender. Drain. Boil *konnyaku* briefly, drain, and julienne cut. Boil watercress briefly and cut in 1-in lengths. Julienne cut cucumber in 1-in lengths, sprinkle with salt, and allow to stand 20 minutes. Wring out moisture.

3.   Make sure ingredients in step *2* are as free as possible of moisture. Immediately before serving, combine with sauce and heap in a bowl.

Salt Herring Roe and Smoked Salmon

Traditionally the Japanese people eat salt herring roe (*kazuno-ko*) as a New Year treat because its numerous individual eggs are supposed to ensure abundant posterity. Cut in small pieces, it has a pleasingly crunchy texture.

    3 oz salt herring roe
    3 oz sliced smoked salmon
    Watercress

1.   Let the herring roe stand in plenty of water in the refrigerator overnight to eliminate almost all of its saltiness. Remove the thin outer membrane with your fingers.

2.   Slice the herring roe diagonally about 1/2 in thick. Dry the slices with paper towels.

3.   Cut the sliced smoked salmon to the same sizes as the herring roe. Combine on a serving plate and garnish with watercress.

Salmon and Tofu Mini-croquettes *(24 croquettes)*

These deep-fried tidbits made of a paste of salmon and tofu should be served hot.

> **1 lb salmon fillet**
> **1 block tofu (*momen*, or cotton tofu is better; a block of Japanese *momen* tofu**
> **weighs about 14 oz)**
> **4 scallions (white part)**
> **2 Tbsp cornstarch**
> **½ tsp salt**
> **2 Tbsp sesame seeds**
> **Oil for frying**
> **Green peppers and watercress for garnish**

1. Prepare the tofu according to the following procedures.
   a. Gently lower tofu into a pan of water. Adjust water so that it barely covers
   . tofu.
   b. Bring water to the boil. Discard hot water. Without breaking it, cool tofu
   in cold water.
   c. Wrap tofu in cheesecloth or paper towel. Put tofu on a chopping board. On
   top of each block, place something weighing about a pound—a dinner plate,
   for instance. Tilt chopping board. Allow tofu to drain for about an hour in
   a cool place. At the conclusion of this period, a block of tofu that originally
   weighed 14 oz will weigh from 9 to 10 oz. If plenty of time is available, tofu
   may be taken from the hot water, put into a deep dish, and cooled in the
   refrigerator from 3 to 4 hours.
2. Chop white parts of scallions in a food processor. Set aside.
3. Skin salmon and remove all bones. Reduce it to a paste in a food processor.
Add tofu, cornstarch, and salt. Continue to mix for a few seconds. Add sesame
seeds.
4. Heat oil to 350°F. Dip a tablespoon into the hot oil and use it to shape salmon-
tofu mixture into balls. Drop them into the hot oil and fry till golden brown.
5. Seed the green peppers and cut into quarters or sixths. Dry with paper towels
and fry briefly in oil.
6. Arrange salmon-tofu croquettes on a serving plate and garnish with fried green
peppers and watercress.

Deep-fried Tofu with Shrimp *(Serves 4 to 6)*

Deep-fried tofu decorated with small shrimp should be served hot.

> **2 blocks tofu *(momen)***
> **12 (4 oz) shrimp (small)**
> **Salt**
> **Pepper**
> **2 tsp sakè**

4 scallions
4 oz *daikon* radish or 8 ordinary radishes
Oil for frying
Flour
White sesame seeds
½ Tbsp soy sauce

1. Boil and drain tofu according to procedures on p. 19.
2. Wash, shell, and devein shrimp. Sprinkle with salt, pepper, and sakè. Allow to stand for 20 minutes.
3. Julienne cut white parts of scallions. Grate *daikon* radish and allow to drain in a colander till it has lost about half its weight.
4. Heat oil for frying in a fairly large, deep pan to 350°F. Cut each block of tofu into 6 equal cubes. Dry with paper towels. Dust lightly with flour and fry till golden brown. Take care tofu cubes do not adhere to each other during frying. Lift out with a slotted spoon and drain on a rack.
5. Dry shrimp well. Dust with flour and fry in the same oil.
6. Arrange tofu in a serving dish. Place a fried shrimp on top of each piece. Sprinkle julienne-cut scallions and white sesame seeds over the top of the tofu. Divide the grated radish into 6 small portions and place 1 on top of each piece of tofu. Season the radish with a few drops of soy sauce.

Fried Smelt with Shrimp *(Serves 4)*

For best results, make all preparations before frying. Do not overcook the shrimp.

20 smelt
12 shrimp (medium)
⅔ tsp salt
¼ cup sakè or sherry
8 radishes
Lemon
Oil for frying
Flour

1. Snap heads from smelt with left hand and remove viscera by running a finger of the right hand through the belly. Wash and drain thoroughly in a colander.
2. Shell shrimp, leaving tail shell intact. Devein. Sprinkle smelt and shrimp with salt and marinate in sakè for 10 minutes.
3. Wash and trim radishes and cut lemon into wedges.
4. Thoroughly dry smelt and shrimp. To ensure removal of all moisture from shrimp-tail shells, cut off the end with a knife and with the knife point jiggle the flesh to allow water to escape.
5. Heat oil to 350°F. Put flour in a small paper bag. Add smelt and shake bag

a few times to coat. Repeat the same process with the shrimp. Fry smelt and shrimp till crisp and golden.

6. Arrange fried smelt and shrimp on a serving plate, sprinkle with salt, and garnish with radishes and lemon wedges.

Fried Shrimp *Gyōza* *(Serves 4)*

Gyōza are Chinese dumplings usually made of chopped meat and vegetables in a pasta wrapping. This variation uses a filling of fine-chopped shrimp and calls for deep frying instead of the usual combination of sautéing and steaming. The filling is delicious fried in tortilla cases too.

> **4 oz unshelled shrimp**
> **$\frac{1}{2}$ oz pork suet (may be omitted)**
> **$\frac{1}{2}$ egg white**
> **Salt**
> **1 Tbsp sakè**
> **1 Tbsp water**
> **20 sheets *gyōza* pasta**
> **Oil for frying**
> **Parsley**
> **Lettuce**

1. Shell and devein shrimp. Chop into a paste with pork suet (a meat grinder or a food processor may be used). Add egg white, salt, sakè, and water. Blend thoroughly.
2. Divide the filling into 20 equal portions. Place one portion on one half of each sheet of *gyōza* pasta. Wet the edge of *gyōza* pasta with water. Fold remaining half of pasta over to conceal filling. Seal edges (with a fork).
3. Heat oil in a deep frying pan to 340° to 350°F. Fry *gyōza* a few at a time till brown. Drain and serve garnished with parsley and lettuce.

Baked Clams *(Serves 4)*

Cutting the black hinge prevents the clams from popping open and wasting their juices. Still be on the safe side and place a pan under them to catch whatever delicious juices might escape. This is an excellent way to include clams in outdoor barbecues. They are done when they begin to steam.

> **8 clams**
> **Lemon or a combination of equal parts lemon juice and soy sauce or a sauce made by combining 2 Tbsp soy sauce, $\frac{1}{4}$ tsp crushed garlic, $\frac{1}{4}$ tsp grated ginger, and 1 tsp chopped scallion**

1.   Wash clams and allow them to stand for half a day in a cool, dark place in salted water (1 Tbsp salt to 1 quart water).

2.   Cut off the black tendon at the hinge of the two halves of the shell. This will prevent the shells from popping open and spilling the delicious juices at baking time.

3.   Heat the oven to 400°F. Place the clams on a cookie sheet or other flat, low-sided pan and cover with a piece of aluminum foil cut to cover an area slightly larger than that occupied by the clams themselves. Crumple the foil slightly. When the clams begin to steam, remove them from the oven.

4.   Serve them with lemon juice or with either of the sauces listed above.

Clams Steamed in Sakè and Butter *(Serves 4)*

To enjoy this simple but delicious dish at its best, assemble ingredients beforehand and cook immediately before serving. Use short-necked or other small clams.

21 oz clams (short-neck or other small clams)
3 scallions
2 Tbsp salad oil
2 Tbsp crushed garlic
2 Tbsp sakè or white wine
2 Tbsp soy sauce
2 Tbsp butter

1.   To cause them to eject sand, allow the clams to stand overnight in plenty of cool, lightly salted water. Wash them under running water, rubbing the shells together in your hands. Drain in a colander. Chop scallions.

2.   Heat oil in a frying pan. Sauté garlic. Remove garlic and reserve.

3.   Add clams to the oil remaining in the pan. Cover the pan and, shaking it gently, sauté over a high heat. When the clams have opened their shells, lower the heat.

4.   Add chopped scallions, sakè, soy sauce, and butter. Toss lightly. The reserved sautéed garlic may be returned to the pan at this time.

Shrimp Fried in Cornmeal *(Serves 4)*

A flowerlike appetizer with the tempting color combination of shrimp pink and cornmeal gold.

> **15 (½ lb) shrimp**
> **Salt**
> **1 Tbsp sakè**
> **Kiwi fruit**
> **1 egg white**
> **Cornstarch**
> **Cornmeal**
> **Oil for frying**
> **Curley endive**
> **Grapefruit sections**
> **Fresh mint**

1. Shell shrimp, leaving tail section of shell intact.
2. Open and devein shrimp. Round them according to instructions on p. 15. Sprinkle with salt and sakè and allow to stand for 20 minutes. Peel and slice kiwi fruit.
3. Lightly beat egg white. Coat open part of shrimp with cornstarch, then in egg white, and finally in cornmeal.
4. In a deep frying pan, heat oil to 325°F. Fry shrimp for about 1 minute or until crisp.
5. Arrange shrimp on a bed of curly endive on a serving plate. Make a border of alternating grapefruit sections and kiwi-fruit slices. Garnish with fresh mint.

Marinated Smelt *(Serves 6)*

The various parts of the fish anatomy—flesh, skin, internal organs, head, and so on—are nutritious in different ways. That is why eating them whole provides maximum nourishment. Although sliced fish tends to be more popular, this way of frying then marinating whole smelt deserves a try. Rainbow trout, cod, salmon, or swordfish may be used in place of smelt.

> **⅔ lb smelt**
> **Flour**
> **2 red chili peppers**
> **5 scallions (white part)**
> **Oil for frying**
> *Marinade:*
> **⅓ cup stock (see pp. 37–39) or chicken broth**
> **⅓ cup rice vinegar**
> **2 Tbsp soy sauce**

    2 Tbsp sakè
    ¹⁄₂ Tbsp sugar
    ¼ tsp salt

1.   Wash smelt and drain in a colander. Put flour in a paper (or plastic) bag. Dry smelt with paper towels. A few at a time, shake in the bag to coat with flour.
2.   Combine marinade ingredients. Soften red chili peppers by soaking in water for a short time. Cut off ends and remove and discard seeds. Slice into thin rings. Slice scallions on the diagonal. Add pepper and scallions to the marinade.
3.   In a deep pan, heat oil to 375°F. Fry smelt, a quarter of the batch at a time, for from 3 to 4 minutes or until crisp.
4.   Lift fried fish from oil and put them into marinade. Allow to stand for from 12 hours to a day. Since they are good even after 2 or 3 days' marinating, it is convenient to prepare these fish in large batches.

Shrimp and *Okara* (Serves 4–6)

To prepare soy milk, from which tofu is made, soybeans are ground, mixed with water, and simmered. The residue left after the milk is poured off is a mash called *okara*. Check with your nearby tofu dealer about its availability.

    ³⁄₄ lb *okara*
    ¹⁄₃ lb shrimp (or scallops)
    4 mushrooms
    ¹⁄₂ cup frozen mixed vegetables
    2 Tbsp sesame oil
    1 Tbsp sugar
    1 Tbsp sakè
    3 Tbsp soy sauce

1.   Place *okara* in boiling water. Return to the boil. Skim off scum. Pour water and *okara* carefully into a colander lined with cheesecloth. Bring edges of towel together and wring to force out as much moisture as possible.
2.   Devein and wash shrimp. Parboil. Drain, reserving enough of the water to make 2 cups.
3.   Slice mushrooms and thaw frozen vegetables. Drain.
4.   Heat sesame oil in a frying pan. Sauté *okara* over a medium heat. Add shrimp and mushrooms and continue sautéing. Combine reserved water, sugar, sakè, and soy sauce. Add to pan and continue sautéing over low heat till mixture is fairly dry. Add mixed vegetables and cook until they are done. Serve in deep individual bowls.

Scrambled Eggs with Scallops and Mixed Vegetables (Serves 4)

    8 eggs
    Salt

Pepper
4 Tbsp milk
8 scallops
8 Tbsp frozen mixed vegetables
2 Tbsp salad oil

1.   Lightly beat eggs in a large bowl. Season with salt and pepper; add milk and beat lightly. Break scallops into fairly large pieces and drain. Add scallops and thawed and drained mixed vegetables to egg mixture. Mix lightly.
2.   Heat salad oil in a frying pan. Pour in eggs and, stirring constantly, cook to desired degree of firmness.

Scrambled Eggs with *Wakame Seaweed* *(Serves 4–6)*

The eggs will be lighter if you use a little more oil. This makes a wholesome and filling breakfast dish.

$\frac{1}{6}$ oz dried *wakame*
6 eggs
$\frac{1}{3}$ tsp salt
Pepper
3 Tbsp salad oil

1.   Wash *wakame*, soften it in water, and julienne cut it. Drain well.
2.   Beat eggs lightly; season with salt and pepper. Add *wakame*.
3.   Heat salad oil in a frying pan. Pour in egg mixture all at once. Over a high heat, stirring constantly with a wide circular movement, cook to desired degree of doneness. Serve at once.

Japanese-style Scrambled Eggs *(Serves 4–6)*

Colorful, simple and appetizing, this dish is best prepared in a non-stick frying pan.

5 eggs
$\frac{1}{4}$ lb shelled, deveined, and boiled shrimp
2 Tbsp stock (pp. 37–39)
2 tsp sugar
1 tsp soy sauce
$\frac{1}{2}$ tsp salt
8 champignons
2 Tbsp salad oil
2 Tbsp green peas

1.   Combine stock, sugar, soy sauce, and salt. Lightly beat eggs and add to these seasonings.

2.   Slice champignons. Heat salad oil in a frying pan. Sauté shrimp and champignons. Add egg mixture and cook over a low heat, stirring 4 or 5 wooden chopsticks held together make a convenient stirring tool—to prevent sticking.
3.   When eggs are about half done, add green peas. Remove pan from heat. Remove eggs to a serving dish at once to prevent overcooking from the heat of the pan.

Marinated Sashimi *(Serves 6 to 8)*

Even people who dislike the idea of eating raw fish find this dish appealing. Add the tomatoes immediately before serving.

> **1 lb sashimi (scallops, halibut, bass, sea bream, or other white-flesh fish)**
> **$\frac{1}{4}$ cup lemon juice**
> **$\frac{1}{4}$ cup lime juice**
> **$\frac{1}{2}$ cup olive oil**
> **$\frac{1}{4}$ cup chopped scallions (white part)**
> **Cayenne pepper**
> **Salt**
> **Pepper**
> **1 tomato, large**
> **Parsley**

1.   Slice large scallops horizontally in 2. Slice sashimi somewhat larger than scallops.
2.   Combine lemon and lime juices. Marinate sashimi in this mixture for 2 hours.
3.   Beat olive oil in a bowl with a wire whip or rotary egg beater. Remove sashimi from marinade and set aside. Slowly add marinade to olive oil, beating constantly. To this dressing, add scallions, cayenne pepper, salt, and pepper.
4.   Marinate the sashimi in this mixture in the refrigerator for from 2 to 3 hours.
5.   Peel, seed, and dice tomato. Add to the marinade and the sashimi.
6.   Heap in a serving bowl and garnish with parsley.

Sashimi Salad with Tostadas *(Serves 4)*

You may use deep-fried spring-roll pasta or even cornflakes in place of the tostadas. Commercially available soy-sauce dressing flavored with sesame oil is good with this dish.

> **1 lb sashimi (tuna, yellowtail, and so on)**
> **4-in section *daikon* radish**
> **1 carrot**
> **1 cucumber**
> **Romaine lettuce**
> **2 tortillas**
> **Oil for frying**

1 oz peanuts
Lemon peel
French dressing

1. Slice fish for sashimi and chill.
2. Julienne cut *daikon* radish, carrot, and cucumber into 2-in lengths. Tear lettuce into bite-size pieces. Dip vegetables in cold water and drain in a colander. Chill.
3. Heat oil in a frying pan to 350°F. Fry tortillas till golden. Drain on paper towels. Coarse crumble tortillas in a plastic bag. Chop peanuts coarse. Julienne cut lemon peel.
4. Heap vegetables in a deep bowl. Top with sashimi. Sprinkle fried tortillas and peanuts over these ingredients. Add lemon peel and top with dressing.

Seaweed Salad *(Serves 4)*

$\frac{1}{5}$ **oz dried** *wakame*
Small amount *tosaka* **seaweed**
Iceberg lettuce
Avocado
Lemon juice
Dressing:
  1 Tbsp salad oil
  1 Tbsp sesame oil
  2 Tbsp soy sauce
  1 Tbsp lemon juice

1. Wash *wakame* thoroughly and soften for 5 to 6 minutes in lukewarm water. Drain in a colander. Plunge first into boiling water and then immediately into cold water. Drain again. Cut into bite-size pieces.
2. Wash *tosaka* seaweed thoroughly and cut into bite-size pieces.
3. Wash lettuce and tear into bite-size pieces. Pit then peel avocado. Dice flesh coarse and sprinkle with lemon juice.
4. Combine salad oil and sesame oil in a mixing bowl. Beating constantly with a rotary beater or wire whip, slowly add soy sauce and lemon juice.
5. Combine lettuce, *wakame*, and *tosaka* seaweed in a salad bowl. Coat with dressing. Sprinkle diced avocado over other ingredients.

Orange Roughy and Pasta Salad *(Serves 4)*

Children are fond of this salad, to which you may add ham or hard-boiled egg for visual appeal. Cod, sea bream, tuna, swordfish, or halibut may be substituted for orange roughy.

$\frac{1}{2}$ **lb orange roughy**
$\frac{1}{4}$ **lb thin-sliced onion**

Salt
Pepper
$\frac{1}{4}$ cup white wine
$\frac{1}{4}$ lb pasta (shell macaroni)
6 radishes
$\frac{1}{4}$ lb thin-sliced cabbage
$\frac{1}{4}$ cup mayonnaise
$\frac{1}{2}$ Tbsp Dijon mustard
$\frac{1}{4}$ cup sliced almonds
Romaine lettuce

1. Spread sliced onions over bottom of a pan, top with fish, and sprinkle with salt and pepper. Sprinkle white wine over fish. Cover tightly and steam till done, taking care not to allow it to burn. Cool and cut into bite-size pieces.
2. Boil and thoroughly drain pasta.
3. Slice radishes and combine with sliced cabbage.
4. Mix mayonnaise and Dijon mustard.
5. Lightly toast sliced almonds in the oven.
6. Combine fish with pasta, vegetables, and mayonnaise mixture and season with salt and pepper.
7. Line a large salad bowl with romaine lettuce, add the salad, and top with toasted sliced almonds.

Shrimp Salad with Strawberry Dressing *(Serves 4)*

The dressing makes this salad extra special.

24 ($\frac{3}{4}$ lb) shrimp (small)
1 orange
Daikon **sprouts or alfalfa sprouts**
Orange peel from $\frac{1}{2}$ orange
Lemon peel from $\frac{1}{2}$ lemon
Curly lettuce
Dressing:
   3 large strawberries
   $\frac{1}{3}$ cup salad oil
   2 Tbsp lemon juice
   $\frac{1}{3}$ tsp salt
   Pepper

1. Devein shrimp, leaving the shells on. Wash and boil till barely done. Peel.
2. Peel orange. Divide flesh in half. Cut off and discard *daikon*-sprout or alfalfa-sprout roots. Cut *daikon* sprouts in half lengthwise. Wash and drain thoroughly.
3. Use only the zest (that is, the thin, outer, colored part) of the orange and lemon peel. Julienne cut it and, after dipping it briefly in boiling water, cool it in cold water to eliminate bitterness.

4. Force strawberries through sieve. In a large bowl, with a wire whip, beat salad oil, gradually adding lemon juice, salt, pepper, and sieved strawberries.

5. Cut curly lettuce into bite-size pieces. Line a large salad bowl with it. Add shrimp, orange flesh, and *daikon* sprouts (or alfalfa sprouts). Sprinkle these ingredients with julienne-cut lemon and orange zest. Top with dressing.

Shrimp and Avocado Salad *(Serves 4)*

This is a filling salad. Prepare the shimp ahead of time and chill them. Chill avocados too but do not peel and slice them until immediately before serving, as they discolor.

> $\frac{1}{2}$ **lb shrimp**
> **3 Tbsp lemon juice**
> **1 Tbsp white wine**
> **Salt**
> **2 hard-boiled eggs**
> **2 avocados**
> **4 Tbsp mayonnaise**
> **3 Tbsp chopped celery**
> **1 Tbsp chopped scallions**

1. Devein shrimp, leaving shells on. Briefly boil them—till they have just turned color—in water seasoned with 1 Tbsp lemon juice, 1 Tbsp white wine, and a little salt. Shell and cut them into 2 or 3 pieces, depending on their sizes.

2. Chop hard-boiled eggs coarse.

3. Taking care not to rip peels, cut avocados in half lengthwise. Remove and discard seeds. Put flesh in a bowl, reserving peels to use as cups to hold the salad. Sprinkle both flesh and peels with lemon juice.

4. Combine the mayonnaise, celery, and scallions. Season avocado flesh with this seasoning. Combine with shrimp. Fill avocado-peel cups with the salad.

The combination of avocado and fish is considered excellent for the health for the following reasons. The EPA in fish and shellfish is said to prevent arteriosclerosis. In the human body, EPA tends to acidify readily. Vitamin E, which prevents such acidification—and is considered a preventative of cardiovascular diseases and other ailments associated with adulthood—is abundant in wheat germ, soybeans, spinach, vegetable oils, and avocados.

Colorful Shrimp Congealed Salad *(Serves 4–6)*

> **12 small shrimp**
> $\frac{2}{5}$ **oz gelatin**
> $\frac{1}{4}$ **cup water**
> $\frac{3}{4}$ **cup boiling water**
> **4 Tbsp chopped onion**

$\frac{1}{3}$ **tsp salt**
$\frac{1}{8}$ **tsp cayenne pepper**
2–3 cucumbers to make 1 cup juice
$\frac{1}{4}$ **cup mayonnaise**
Lettuce

1. Without removing shells, devein shrimp. Boil only till they change color. Shell.
2. Soften gelatin in water. Add boiling water and stir to dissolve gelatin completely. Add chopped onion, salt, and cayenne pepper.
3. Grate cucumbers. Strain to make 1 cup juice. Reserve cucumber flesh. Combine cucumber juice and gelatin mixture. Spread shrimp in the bottom of a wet mold. Gently pour the gelatin mixture on top and chill till set.
4. Combine cucumber flesh and mayonnaise.
5. Make a bed of lettuce on a serving dish. Dip mold in warm water. Invert over lettuce. Remove mold. Garnish salad with mayonnaise-cucumber dressing.

Crab Meat and Cucumbers with Lemon Soy Sauce *(Serves 4)*

Although this salad is more colorful made with crab meat, you may substitute flaked, boiled white fish or thin-sliced scallops or abalone.

6 oz cooked crab legs
1 tsp lemon juice
2 Japanese-style cucumbers
$\frac{1}{2}$ **tsp salt**
Lemon Soy Sauce:
2 Tbsp lemon juice
$\frac{1}{2}$ **tsp soy sauce**

1. Shell and pick over the crab to remove all bony membranes. Separate meat with a fork and sprinkle it with 1 tsp lemon juice.
2. Wash cucumbers and slice into thin rounds. Sprinkle with salt and allow to stand for 20 minutes. When cucumbers are wilted, wring them firmly in the hands.
3. Combine crab meat and cucumbers in a bowl. Mix lemon soy sauce ingredients and pour them over the salad. Salt to taste. Serve in individual bowls.

Caesar Salad with White-flesh Fish *(Serves 4)*

$\frac{1}{3}$ **lb fillet of white-flesh fish**
Flour
Oil for frying
1 cup croutons
$\frac{1}{2}$ **head iceberg lettuce**
2 hard-boiled eggs
French Dressing:
2 Tbsp rice vinegar or lemon juice

Salt
Pepper
Mustard
6 Tbsp salad oil
1 Tbsp capers
1 Tbsp chopped parsley

1.   Cut fish into bite-size pieces, lightly coat with flour, and fry till golden brown in oil heated to 350°F.
2.   To make croutons, cut sliced bread into 1/3-in cubes and toast till golden brown in a moderate oven. Wash lettuce, drain, and tear into bite-size pieces. Chill. Coarse chop eggs.
3.   Combine vinegar, salt, pepper, and mustard. Beating with a rotary egg beater or wire whip, slowly add oil. Add remaining dressing ingredients.
4.   Lightly coat fish and lettuce with dressing. Sprinkle eggs and croutons over the top of the salad. Serve at once.

Seafood-and-seed Salad Topping

This combination of delicacies from sea and land is a flavorsome topping for impromptu salads. It is delicious on hot, steamed rice too.

$\frac{1}{4}$ cup *jako* (small dried fish)
$\frac{1}{4}$ cup pine nuts
$\frac{1}{4}$ cup shaved dried bonito *(kezuribushi)*
$\frac{1}{4}$ cup powdered seaweed *(aonori)*
$\frac{1}{4}$ cup sesame seeds
1 tsp salt

1.   Toast the *jako* and pine nuts in an oven (220°F) for from 5 to 6 minutes. Cool.
2.   Combine all ingredients in a jar and shake well to mix.
3.   Use this mixture as a savory addition to green salads or as a topping for hot steamed rice.
    Store in the refrigerator and use as quickly as convenient.

Jako and Cabbage Salad *(Serves 4)*

The dried tiny white fish called *jako* may be bought in bulk, frozen, and used as needed. They are very versatile.

2 oz *jako*
$\frac{3}{4}$ lb cabbage
1 Japanese-style cucumber
4 radishes
1 stalk celery

2 Tbsp salad oil
Dressing:
   4 Tbsp salad oil
   2 Tbsp sesame oil
   1 Tbsp soy sauce

1.   Cut cabbage into julienne strips about 1 1/2 by 1/2 in. Dip into boiling water for 20 or 30 seconds. Drain thoroughly.
2.   Slice cucumbers diagonally into thin slices. Slice radishes and celery stalk crosswise.
3.   Heat salad oil and sauté *jako* in it for about 30 seconds.
4.   Using a wire whip or rotary egg beater, combine dressing ingredients.
5.   Combine *jako* and all vegetables in a salad bowl. Add dressing and toss.

Jako and *Daikon* Salad *(Serves 4)*

Jako are especially nutritious because, eaten whole, they are a good source of calcium.

   2 oz *jako*
   ⅓ lb *daikon* **radish**
   1 carrot
   1 Japanese-style cucumber
   ½ tsp salt
   2 Tbsp salad oil
   1 Tbsp white sesame seeds

1.   Peel carrot and *daikon* radish and cut them into julienne strips about 1 1/2 in. long. Wash cucumber and cut it into similar strips. Combine these three ingredients, sprinkle them with salt, and allow them to stand for about 30 minutes. Squeeze as much moisture as possible from them and chill them. (Some graters have blades that produce julienne strips.)
2.   Heat salad oil and sauté *jako* in it for from 4 to 5 seconds.
3.   Combine vegetables and *jako*, together with the oil in which it was cooked. Mix well and put into a salad bowl.
4.   Top with a sprinkling of white sesame seeds.

Note: Results are better if the vegetables are squeezed once more immediately before being combined with the oil and *jako*. If making the salad in advance, prepare the vegetables as in step *1*. But do not sauté the *jako* until immediately before serving time.

Jako and Rice Salad *(Serves 4 to 6)*

   2 oz (1 cup) *jako*
   3 cups steamed rice (preferably cooked slightly hard)
   1 Japanese-style cucumber

2 oz cheese (Monterey Jack or Camembert)
2 hard-boiled eggs
Lettuce
2 Tbsp toasted sesame seeds
¼ cup French dressing

1. Dry *jako* for about 5 minutes in an oven preheated to 225°F. Dice cucumbers and cheese fine. Cut eggs into wedges. Wash lettuce and tear it into bite-size pieces.
2. Line a large salad bowl with lettuce. Combine and add all other ingredients except eggs.
3. Garnish with egg wedges.

Squid Salad *(Serves 4)*

2 squid
½ head iceberg lettuce
2 hard-boiled eggs
1 clove garlic
Salt
1 Tbsp capers
⅓ cup chopped English walnuts
Dressing:
½ cup mayonnaise
¼ cup olive oil
1 Tbsp lemon juice
1 tsp mustard
Pepper

1. Clean squid (see p. 133). Wash. Cut into rings 1/3 in thick. Cut tentacles into bite-size pieces. Parboil.
2. Wash lettuce, tear into bite-size pieces, and chill. Coarse chop eggs.
3. Mix dressing ingredients thoroughly.
4. Rub sides of a salad bowl with peeled garlic clove and sprinkle with salt.
5. Lightly coat lettuce and squid with dressing and arrange in salad bowl; sprinkle with capers and egg. Top with walnuts and serve at once.

A Salad of *Wakame* and Canned Tuna *(Serves 4)*

A colorful, low-calorie salad.

2 Tbsp dried, cut *wakame*
2 Japanese-style cucumbers
1 carrot
1 stalk celery
½ onion, medium
4 radishes

6 oz canned tuna (water-packed)
Dressing:
  1 Tbsp salad oil
  1 Tbsp sesame oil
  2 Tbsp soy sauce
  1 Tbsp lemon juice

1. Sprinkle dried, cut *wakame* on the surface of water in a bowl and allow it to stand for 5 minutes. Drain well in a colander. Cut cucumber, carrot, and celery in julienne strips about 1 1/2 in long. Slice onion thin and allow it to stand in cold water for about 20 minutes. Wring moisture from it. Slice radishes thin. Drain canned tuna. Chill all ingredients.
2. Combine salad oil and sesame oil in a bowl. Constantly beating with a wire whip or a rotary egg beater, add soy sauce and lemon juice.
3. Arrange vegetables in a salad bowl with *wakame* in the middle. Top *wakame* with canned tuna.
4. Pour on dressing at the table.

Cooked, boned, cold chicken meat may be used in place of the canned tuna. To prepare, sprinkle chicken with salt, pepper, 2 Tbsp sakè, and a little water and steam. When it is done and cool, separate meat with your fingers.

The dressing keeps well in the refrigerator and may be made in quantity.

Salad of *Wakame*, Dried Shrimp, and *Daikon* Sprouts *(Serves 4)*

The piquancy of the *daikon* sprouts and the fragrance of the sesame oil make this salad distinctive.

  $\frac{1}{3}$ oz dried *wakame*
  1 pack *daikon* sprouts
  $\frac{1}{4}$ cup dried shrimp *(sakura-ebi)*
  1 Tbsp sesame seeds
  2 Tbsp French dressing

1. Wash *wakame* and soften in lukewarm water for 5 to 6 minutes. Drain in a colander. Next plunge it into boiling water then immediately into cold water. Once again drain in a colander. Cut into bite-size pieces.
2. Cut off and discard *daikon*-sprout roots. Cut in half, wash, and drain.
3. Wash briefly and drain dried shrimp.
4. Place seeds in a heavy, lidded, unoiled frying pan. Over a moderate heat, toast seeds, shaking the pan constantly. When 2 or 3 of the seeds pop, like popcorn, remove the pan from the heat. Cool.

Toast seeds in quantity and, after they have cooled, store them for ready use in a jar with a tight-fitting lid. The fragrance of the seeds may be increased by crushing them between layers of kitchen wrap with a rolling pin. Pretoasted sesame seeds are available in markets.

5.   Combine *wakame*, dried shrimp, and *daikon* sprouts in a bowl. Add French dressing and toss. Top with a sprinkling of toasted sesame seeds.

Udon-noodle Salad *(Serves 4)*

The base of the salad is chilled *udon* noodles. Feel free to vary the other ingredients to suit your tastes.

>   **2 packages *udon* noodles**
>   **¼ oz dried *wakame***
>   **½ cup canned tuna**
>   **1 stalk celery**
>   **2 tomatoes**
>   **Watercress**
>   **½ cup frozen canned corn**
>   **2 Tbsp sesame seeds**
> *Dressing:*
>   **2 Tbsp soy sauce**
>   **1 Tbsp vinegar**
>   **1 Tbsp salad oil**
>   **1 Tbsp sesame oil**
>   **Pepper**

1.   Boil noodles in plenty of water until just tender. Drain in a colander. Chill.
2.   Soften *wakame* in water. Dip briefly in boiling water. Cut into bite-size pieces. Drain. Break tuna into coarse pieces. Julienne cut celery into short strips. Slice tomato into wedges. Cut watercress into convenient lengths. Drain canned corn. Toast sesame seeds.
3.   Combine soy sauce and vinegar. Beating constantly with a rotary beater or wire whip, add salad oil slowly. Still beating, add sesame oil and season with pepper.
4.   Combine noodles, tuna, *wakame*, celery, tomato, watercress, and corn in a salad bowl. Add dressing and top with toasted sesame seeds.

Sea-delicacies Salad *(Serves 4)*

The combination of soy sauce and garlic is a perfect accent for this colorful collection of delicacies from the sea.

>   **½ lb fillet of white-flesh fish (cod, bass, halibut, and so on)**
>   **½ cup white wine**
>   **Salt**
>   **Pepper**
>   **Bay leaf**
>   **Celery leaf**
>   **⅓ lb squid (skinned and cleaned)**

4 unshelled shrimp
$\frac{1}{3}$ **oz dried** *wakame*
$\frac{1}{2}$ **head iceberg lettuce**
8 radishes
Dressing:
  2 Tbsp vinegar
  $\frac{1}{2}$ **tsp salt**
  $\frac{1}{2}$ **Tbsp soy sauce**
  Pepper
  4 Tbsp salad oil
  1 Tbsp sesame oil
  $\frac{1}{2}$ **tsp crushed garlic**

1. In a deep saucepan combine white-flesh fish, 1/4 cup white wine, salt, pepper, bay leaf, and celery leaf. Add water to cover and simmer briefly.

2. Cut squid into bite-size pieces and add to pan with fish. Add 1/4 cup white wine and boil briefly. Drain in a colander.

3. Without shelling, devein shrimp. Boil in salted water until they change color. Drain. Shell, leaving the tail-section shell intact.

4. Soften *wakame* in water. Cut into bite-size pieces. Parboil. Immediately plunge into ice water. Drain in a colander.

5. Wash lettuce and tear it into bite-size pieces. Slice radishes.

6. Combine vinegar, salt, soy sauce, and pepper. Beating constantly with a rotary beater or a wire whip, slowly add salad oil and sesame oil. Finally add garlic.

7. Coat all ingredients with dressing and mount in a salad bowl.

Soups and Savory Custards

Halibut and Shrimp Savory
Custard (*Chawan-mushi*) (p. 48)

Japanese soups, or *shirumono*, may be divided into two major categories, both of which use a basic stock (*dashi*) most often made from a combination of *kombu* and shaved dried bonito (*kezuribushi*). In one category, fish or vegetables are served in clear stock. The other kind of soup is flavored with bean paste or miso.

● *About Basic Stock*

As important to Japanese food as chicken stock is to Western cooking, *dashi*, or basic stock, made of *kombu* and shaved dried bonito, is the starting point of many different kinds of food. *Ichiban-dashi*, or first stock, is most delicately flavored and is used in clear soups. To prepare it, ingredients are cooked very briefly. The ingredients used in making first stock may be reused and cooked longer to produce second stock, or *niban-dashi*.

● *Making Stock*

The two methods listed below are traditional. With method A, sufficient stock for from 4 to 6 persons can be prepared in 20 minutes. *Kombu* and shaved bonito flakes may be stored in the freezer or refrigerator for use whenever needed. But many Japanese housewives and restaurants now prefer the speed and convenience of granular and liquid instant stock bases.

4 cups water
1 4-in square *kombu*
$\frac{1}{2}$ oz shaved, dried bonito flakes

Preparation of First Stock

Method A

1.   Wipe both sides of *kombu* with paper towels, taking care not to wipe away the white powdery substance which gives body to the stock.

2.   Combine water and *kombu* in a saucepan and allow to stand for 10 minutes. Remove *kombu* immediately before water reaches the boil. Lower heat to low.

3.   Add bonito flakes. Turn off heat when liquid returns to the boil. Wait about a minute until bonito flakes sink to the bottom of the pan. Strain through cheese-cloth to obtain a clear stock. The *kombu* and bonito flakes may be retained for use in making second stock.

   Hints: Unless *kombu* is removed before water boils, the flavor will be too strong. Similarly, turn off the heat the minute the liquid reaches a boil the second time or the bonito will impart too strong a flavor.

Wipe both sides of the *kombu* with paper towels.

Add the *kombu* to the cold water before turning on the heat.

Remove the *kombu* immediately before the water boils.

Add the bonito flakes all at once. When the water returns to the boil, immediately turn off the heat.

Strain gently through cloth. Do not wring the cloth.

Method B
1.   Combine water and *kombu* in a saucepan and allow to stand for 2 hours if the temperature is 86°F and for 3 hours if it is 50°F. The stock obtained in this heatless way is delicious enough to use as it is. Or bonito flakes may be added to it. It is then heated only to the boiling point. Then the heat is immediately turned off. The liquid is strained through cheesecloth or a strainer to produce a clear stock.

Preparation of Second Stock

To the bonito and *kombu* used in the preceding recipe, add 3 1/2 cups of water. Bring to a boil and cook for 3 minutes. Turn off the heat and strain. This stock is unacceptable for clear broths but may be used in miso soups or in the preparation of a wide variety of simmered foods.

(1)   Clear Broth

Season 4 cups of first stock with 3/4 tsp salt and 1/2 tsp soy sauce. Prepare whatever vegetables you have in mind and place them in individual soup bowls. Add the broth piping hot and improve the aroma of the soup with fine julienne strips of ginger root or lemon zest. Natural liquids like clam juice may be heated and seasoned with sakè and salt for a delicious broth.

(2)   Miso Soup (*Misoshiru*)

In a saucepan combine basic stock (either first or second stock) and whatever vegetables or other foods you intend to include. Cook till the ingredients are 80 percent done then flavor with miso. Do this by blending the miso with a small amount of stock in a small bowl and then adding this to the soup pot.

Miso differs in flavor and saltiness from region to region, and blending types in soup is considered a good idea. Miso soups require no additional salt. For soup either the dark or medium varieties of miso are preferred. The pale, so-called white, variety is too bland.

Miso soup should never be boiled too long. Blend the miso with liquid outside the pot, add it, then remove the pot from the heat the minute the boiling point has been reached.

The amount of miso required varies with the flavor and salt content, although a general rule of thumb is a lump of miso about the size of a small cherry for each portion of soup.

Seafood gains aroma and miso soup gains richness when the two are combined. Before adding fish to miso soup, boil it briefly to reduce fishy odor. Miso soup goes well, not only with traditional rice, but also with bread and is an excellent addition to the diets of people concerned about blood-cholesterol levels. The soy protein in miso is easily digested. Furthermore, the oil in soy products helps prevent deposition of cholesterol.

(3)   *Chawan-mushi* (Savory Custard)

This delicate custard is sometimes used as a substitute for soup in Japanese meals.

Shrimp, bamboo shoot, and other vegetables and seafoods are cut into appropriate sizes and flavored. They are then placed in individual, heat-proof dishes, into which is poured a seasoned combination of stock and egg. The dishes are covered, and the custards are steamed. This refreshing, delicate custard is beloved by young and old alike. In hot weather, it is delicious served cold.

A Japanese-style steamer, with a lower section for the water and an upper section with a perforated floor for the articles to be steamed, is very useful in preparing dishes of this kind. If the individual dishes lack lids, cover them with cloth or aluminum foil, taking care to avoid contact between the foil and the egg mixture.

At first, with the steamer lid firmly in place, steam at a high heat for 1 or 2 minutes. Then, cracking the lid a little, steam at moderate or low heat for from 15 to 17 minutes. Test by inserting a bamboo skewer into the center of a custard. It is done if the liquid that oozes from it is perfectly clear. This book contains an explanation for a way to make such custards in an ordinary oven, without an oriental steamer.

Swordfish Soup *(Serves 4)*

Ingredients may be varied to suit what you have on hand. You may use commercially prepared mixed vegetables or cauliflower or broccoli. Fry swordfish only until it is crisp on the outside. Do not overcook. If you fry the fish well in advance of serving time, reheat it in an oven. You may substitute bass, bonito, cod, halibut, mackerel, horse mackerel, orange roughy, sea bream, sole, salmon, trout, or yellowtail for swordfish.

> $\frac{1}{2}$ **lb fresh swordfish**
> **Salt**
> **Pepper**
> **Cornstarch**
> **Oil for frying**
> $\frac{1}{2}$ **lb (if frozen, 4 oz) spinach**
> **1 tomato**
> **4 cups chicken broth**

1. Slice swordfish into 20 rectangular slices. Sprinkle with salt and pepper and allow to stand in a colander for 20 minutes. Coat with cornstarch. Heat oil to 350°F and fry fish till crisp on the outside.
2. Wash spinach, boil it briefly, and squeeze out as much moisture as possible. Cut into 1-in lengths. Seed tomato and dice fine. Drain in a colander.
3. Season chicken broth with salt and pepper to taste and bring to a boil. Add diced tomato.
4. Arrange swordfish and spinach in individual soup plates. Ladle in soup.

Shrimp and *Harusame* Broth *(Serves 4)*

Served cold, this is refreshing in hot summer weather.

> **2 oz *harusame* noodles**
> **4 fresh *shiitake* mushrooms**
> **8 small shrimp**
> **Daikon-radish sprouts**
> ***Broth:***
> **4 cups stock (pp. 37–39)**
> **1 Tbsp sakè**
> **⅓ tsp salt**
> **¼ tsp soy sauce**

1. Combine stock, sakè, salt, and soy sauce in a deep saucepan. Bring to a boil. Chill in refrigerator.
2. Cut *harusame* noodles into 5-in lengths. Soften in hot water and drain in a colander. Remove and discard mushroom stems. Toast lightly. Without shelling, devein shrimp. Boil in salted water only until they change color. Shell, leaving tail-section shell intact. Chill all ingredients.
3. Arrange shrimp, mushrooms, and noodles in individual bowls. Add chilled broth and garnish with *daikon*-radish sprouts.

Oyster and Spinach Soup *(Serves 4)*

For this simple soup, select small oysters. Frozen spinach is convenient when you are in a hurry. Since oysters are rich in taurin, which lowers blood-cholesterol levels, this soup is both good and good for you.

> **5 oz oysters**
> **3 oz spinach (2 oz if frozen)**
> **2 eggs**
> **4½ cups stock (pp. 37–39) or chicken broth**
> **½ tsp salt**

1. Wash oysters in running cold water and remove particles of shell if any remain. Drain in a colander.
2. Wash spinach and boil it briefly. Squeeze out as much moisture as possible and cut it into 1-in lengths. Frozen spinach needs only to be thawed. Lightly beat eggs.
3. In a large soup pot, over a medium heat, bring stock, or broth, to the boil. When the boiling point has been reached, drop in the oysters. Simmer for 2 or 3 minutes, skimming off scum as it forms. Salt to taste.
4. Spread the spinach on top of the oysters. Return to the boil. Gently cover the spinach with the beaten egg. Put the lid on the pot and simmer over a low heat for from 30 seconds to a minute. Overcooking toughens the eggs.

Egg-drop Soup with Red Caviar *(Serves 4)*

A luxurious soup that is as beautiful as it is delicious.

> **4 cups chicken broth**
> **¾ tsp salt**
> **Pepper**
> **1½ Tbsp cornstarch**
> **4 Tbsp water**
> **2 eggs**
> **2 tsp sesame oil**
> **2 oz red caviar**
> **Chopped parsley**

1. Bring chicken broth to a boil in a deep pot. Season with salt and pepper. Dissolve cornstarch in water and, stirring constantly, add to broth. Stir till slightly thickened.
2. Lightly beat eggs. Bring soup to boil again and remove from heat. Add beaten eggs. Stir once vigorously with a ladle. Add sesame oil.
3. Pour into individual bowls. Place a small amount of red caviar in the center of each bowl and garnish with chopped parsley. Serve hot.

Clam Broth *(Serves 4)*

The delicate flavors of broth—either traditional Japanese stock or chicken broth—and clams complement each other. Clams are another of those shellfish that lower blood-cholesterol levels because they are rich in taurin.

> **14 (1 lb) clams (small)**
> **2-in length celery**
> **1 3-in square *kombu***
> **4 cups water or chicken broth**
> **¼ tsp salt**
> **¼ tsp soy sauce**

1. Allow clams to eject sand by leaving them to stand in a cool, dark place, in salted water (1/2 Tbsp salt to 2 pints water) for half a day.
2. Julienne cut celery.
3. Wipe both sides of *kombu* with paper towels. Scrub clams well. Combine water (or chicken broth), *kombu*, and clams in a deep soup pot over a medium heat.
4. Remove *kombu* immediately before the water boils. When clams have all opened, remove from the heat. Skim off scum. Rinse each clam in the broth in the pot to make sure no sand remains. Transfer clams to another bowl. Gently pour the top of the broth in the pot into the same bowl, leaving the dregs. Wash the pot. Return clams and broth to the now clean pot. Salt to taste.

5.   Over a medium heat, return to the boil. Season with soy sauce and remove from heat.
6.   Serve in individual bowls garnished with julienne-cut celery.

Note: Do not overcook. The clams are done when the shells have opened.

Creamed Clam and Corn Soup *(Serves 4)*

Easily made with canned ingredients, this is a heartwarming soup for a winter night.

> 3 cups chicken broth
> 1 can (6½ oz) canned chopped clams
> ½ lb canned cream-style corn
> 1 tsp salt
> Pepper
> 4 Tbsp milk
> 2 egg whites
> 1½ Tbsp cornstarch
> 3 Tbsp water
> 2 tsp sesame oil
> Parsley

1.   Combine chicken broth, clams, and corn. Bring to the boil. Season with salt and pepper. Add milk. Lightly beat egg whites.
2.   Lower heat. Dissolve cornstarch in water. Add to the soup, stirring until the mixture thickens. Add sesame oil.
3.   Return to the boil. Turn heat off. Add egg whites at once. Stir vigorously once with a ladle.
4.   Pour into individual serving bowls, garnish with parsley, and serve hot.

Note: Have all ingredients assembled and ready and make the soup quickly.

Miso Soup with Shrimp and Yellowtail *(Serves 4)*

As long as it is fresh, practically any fish is good in this delicious seafood-flavored soup. It is good made with either water or stock.
     You may substitute cod, halibut, mackerel, horse mackerel, salmon, bonito, or sea bream for the yellowtail.

> 4 cups water
> 1 3-in square *kombu* (optional)
> 12 unshelled shrimp (small)
> 4 oz fillet of yellowtail
> 2 scallions

44

2 Tbsp miso (dark red or the lighter variety)

1. Wipe both sides of *kombu* with paper towels. Place *kombu* in a deep soup pan and add water. Devein shrimp. Slice yellowtail into 8 slices. Add shrimp and yellowtail to the soup pan. Chop scallions.
2. Over a low heat, bring contents of the pot to a boil, skimming off scum as it forms and removing the *kombu* immediately before the boiling point is reached. Simmer for about a minute. Remove from heat. Remove shrimp; devein them, leaving the tail shell intact, and return to the pot.
3. In a small bowl, using a rotary egg beater or wire whip, blend miso to a smooth paste with some of the stock from the pot. Add this paste to the pot and return it to the heat.
4. When the soup begins to boil, remove the pot from the heat. Serve in individual bowls with a sprinkling of chopped scallion. A drop or two of juice squeezed from grated ginger adds interest, as does either pepper or chili.

Miso Soup with Short-neck Clams (*Asari*) *(Serves 4)*

Short-neck clams, like other shellfish, go well with miso. But, since they are salty in themselves, the amount of miso used must be reduced. When you are in a hurry, a tasty miso soup can be made by thinning the liquor from canned chopped clams with water and instant stock, heating the liquid with the clams, and flavoring with miso.

2 cups short-neck clams
3 scallions
4 cups water (or stock)
2 Tbsp miso (dark red or the lighter variety)

1. Allow clams to stand half a day in a cool dark place in just enough salted water (1 Tbsp salt to 1 quart water) to cover. Wash well. Chop scallions.
2. Combine water and clams in a deep soup pot and bring to a boil. When clams begin to open, turn the heat off. Skim off scum. When clams are completely open, check for sand. If any is present, rinse clams in the broth in the pot, transfer them to another bowl, then gently pour the top broth from the pot into the same bowl. Discard the dregs and wash the pot. Return clams and broth to the pot.
3. In a small bowl, combine miso and some of the broth. Blend to a smooth paste with a wire whip or a rotary egg beater. Add to the clams and broth.
4. Return to the bowl. The moment the boiling point is reached, remove the pot from the heat and add chopped scallions. Skim off scum.

Miso soup should never be boiled too long. Blend the miso with liquid outside the pot, add it, then remove the pot from the heat the minute the boiling point has been reached.

Miso Soup with *Wakame* and Tofu *(Serves 4)*

Because of its low salt content, this healthful, classic Japanese miso soup goes well with bread as well as rice and is especially popular for breakfast.

> 1⅓ Tbsp dried, cut *wakame*
> ½ block tofu
> 2 scallions
> 4 cups stock (pp. 37–39) (or chicken broth)
> 3 Tbsp miso (red)

1. Soften dried, cut *wakame* in water and drain in a colander. Chop scallions. Cut tofu into 1/3-in dice.
2. Heat stock in a deep soup pot. In a small bowl, with a wire whip or rotary egg beater, blend miso and some of the stock from the pot into a smooth paste. Add to the pot. Add tofu.
3. Bring the soup to the boil, add the *wakame*, and remove from the heat at once. Serve in individual bowls with a sprinkling of chopped scallions.

   As is said in Ingredients, *wakame* is marketed in 3 different varieties. The dried and cut variety used in this recipe is the most convenient.

   This recipe calls for only half a block of tofu. The remainder will keep for several days in fresh water in the refrigerator if the water is changed daily.

Kenchinjiru *(Serves 4)*

This healthful soup was brought home to Japan long ago by Zen priests who had traveled to China to study. First vegetables and tofu are sautéed. Fish or chicken is then added, and the ingredients are simmered in the stock.

> ½ block tofu
> 2 oz carrot
> ⅓ block *konnyaku* (devil's tongue jelly)
> 2 oz burdock
> 4 oz salmon fillet
> 4 scallions
> 2 Tbsp salad oil
> 4 cups stock or chicken broth (Either prepare stock yourself according to the direction on pp. 37–39 or use commercially available granular or liquid stock bases.)
> 1 Tbsp soy sauce
> ¼ tsp salt
> Chili pepper

1. Wash and crumble tofu into fairly large pieces. Drain for 30 minutes in a colander. Cut carrot into 1 1/2-in julienne strips. Boil *konnyaku* for about 30 seconds, wash in cold water, and cut into similar julienne strips. Scrape burdock,

cut it into similar julienne strips, and allow it to stand for a while in cold water. Cut salmon into bite-size pieces. Chop the scallions.

2. Heat oil in a deep pot. In the oil, sauté tofu first. Then add carrots, *konnyaku*, and drained burdock. Sauté for 3 minutes.

3. Add stock or chicken broth, soy sauce, and salt. When liquid comes to the boil, add salmon and simmer for about 20 minutes, or until all the vegetables are tender. Sprinkle with chopped scallions immediately before serving. A dash of chili pepper is a delicious addition.

Noppei-jiru *(Serves 4)*

Noppei means a liquid that has been thickened and is smooth and creamy in texture. This soup is very warming and filling. Yellowtail or mackerel may be substituted for salmon.

> 2 oz carrot
> ⅓ block *konnyaku* (devil's tongue jelly)
> 4 oz potato
> 4 oz salmon
> 2 oz burdock
> 4 cups stock (pp. 37–39)
> 1 Tbsp sakè
> ½ tsp salt
> 1 Tbsp soy sauce
> 1 Tbsp cornstarch
> 2 Tbsp water
> Chili pepper (optional)

1. Wash carrot and cut into 1/3-in rounds. Boil *konnyaku* for 30 seconds, wash in cold water, drain, and cut into bite-size pieces about 1/3 in thick. Peel potato and cut into similar bite-size pieces. Skin and bone salmon and cut it into bite-size pieces. Scrape burdock and cut it into julienne strips 1 1/2 in long. Allow it to stand in cold water for a while.

2. In a soup pot, bring stock to a boil and add sakè. Add vegetables and fish. Simmer until ingredients are tender, about 20 minutes. Five minutes before the conclusion of cooking time, season with salt and soy sauce. Remove from the heat. Blend cornstarch and water. Add to the pot. Return soup to heat and, stirring constantly, bring to a boil. Remove from heat at once. A dash of chili pepper adds interesting piquancy.

Yellowtail and mackerel should be sliced into bite-size pieces and dipped into boiling water before being added to the soup pot.

Shrimp and Chicken Savory Custard (*Chawan-mushi*) *(Serves 4)*

The flavors of shrimp and chicken are sealed inside this delicate custard, which is delicious either hot or, in summertime, cold.

8 shrimp (small)
4 oz chicken meat
Salt
2 Tbsp sakè or sherry
2 Tbsp green peas (frozen)
4 eggs
2 cups chicken broth
⅔ tsp salt
⅓ Tbsp chopped parsley (optional)

1.   Leaving the tail shell intact, shell shrimp. Devein them. Slice chicken meat into 8 slices. Sprinkle both shrimp and chicken with salt and sakè and allow to stand for 20 minutes. Thaw frozen green peas and press them gently to reduce moisture.
2.   Lightly beat eggs, frothing them as little as possible, and combine them with chicken broth and 2/3 tsp salt.
3.   Dry shrimp and chicken meat. Divide these ingredients and the green peas among 4 oven-proof custard cups. Fill each cup with the egg mixture and cover with aluminum foil.
4.   Preheat the oven to 300°F. Bake the custards in the oven for 18 minutes. Remove and allow to stand covered for 5 minutes. Remove the aluminum foil and sprinkle with chopped parsley.

Note: The seafood, vegetables, and egg mixture may be cooked in 1 casserole; and the custard may be divided at the table.

Crab and Asparagus Savory Custard (*Chawan-mushi*) *(Serves 4)*

2 oz crab leg meat
4 spears asparagus (frozen)
1 tsp dried, cut *wakame*
4 eggs
2 cups stock (pp. 37–39) or chicken broth
⅔ tsp salt

1.   Separate crab meat. Thaw asparagus spears and cut them in 1-in lengths. Dry thoroughly. Soften *wakame* in water, drain, and squeeze out as much moisture as possible.
2.   Lightly beat eggs, frothing them as little as possible. Gently blend them with stock or chicken broth and salt.
3.   Divide crab meat, asparagus, and *wakame* among 4 heat-proof custard cups (or cook in 1 casserole). Fill with egg mixture and cover each cup with aluminum foil.
4.   Preheat oven to 300°F. Bake custards for 18 minutes. Remove and allow to stand covered for 5 minutes. Remove aluminum foil and serve.

Halibut and Shrimp Savory Custard (*Chawan-mushi*) *(Serves 4)*

You may substitute bass, sea bream, cod, or orange roughy for the halibut.

> **4 oz fillet of halibut**
> **8 shrimp (small)**
> **Salt**
> **2 Tbsp sakè or sherry**
> **4 Tbsp frozen mixed vegetables**
> **Lemon peel**
> **4 eggs**
> **⅔ tsp salt**
> **2 cups stock (pp. 37–39) or chicken broth**

1.   Slice halibut into 8 slices. Leaving the tail shell intact, shell shrimp. Devein them. Sprinkle shrimp and halibut with salt and sakè and allow them to stand for 20 minutes. Thaw mixed vegetables and press them lightly with the hands to reduce moisture. Cut small (1/2 in diameter) circles of lemon peel (zest only).
2.   Lightly beat eggs, frothing them as little as possible. Gently blend them with salt and stock or chicken broth.
3.   Divide shrimp, halibut, and vegetables among 4 heat-proof custard cups (or cook in 1 casserole). Fill with egg mixture and cover each cup with aluminum foil.
4.   Preheat oven to 300°F. Bake custards for 18 minutes. Remove and allow to stand covered for 5 minutes. Remove aluminum foil, top each with a circle of lemon peel, and serve.

Nabemono (One-dish Meals)

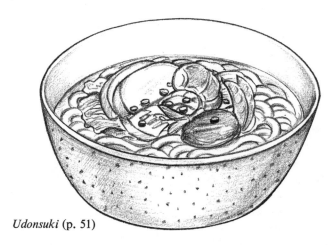

Udonsuki (p. 51)

Nabemono, one-dish meals consisting of a wide variety of different ingredients and generally cooked at the table, are especially popular for congenial gatherings on cold winter evenings. One of the most famous of all these filling dishes, *chirinabe* is to the Japanese cuisine what bouillabaisse is to the French. It consists of vegetables and seafood simmered in Japanese-style stock (*dashi*). When done, the ingredients are removed from the casserole by the diners themselves and dipped in a sauce of equal parts of soy sauce and the juice of some citrus fruit (traditionally the highly aromatic *yuzu* citron). Finally, cooked rice (which has been washed in cold water to reduce its cohesiveness) is added to the liquid remaining in the casserole and heated as a kind of gruel. (Sometimes *udon* noodles are used in place of the rice.)

You are at liberty to select whatever ingredients are desired for the various different kinds of Japanese *nabemono*, which are prepared in ceramic, iron, or copper pots at the table. Additional seasonings must be on hand to prevent the flavor of the broth from weakening during the cooking process.

Yosenabe *(Serves 4)*

The more kinds of seafood used in this delicious casserole meal, the better. Do not feel limited to the ingredients listed below but assemble (the Japanese verb *yoseru* means to gather together, hence the name of the dish) as many seafoods as are available. When everything has been eaten, simmer *udon* noodles in the liquor remaining in the pot.

2 lbs of the following: shrimp, shellfish, squid, cod, halibut, orange roughy, chicken
10 leaves Chinese cabbage or cabbage

2 carrots
8 scallions
4 oz bamboo shoots (canned)
8 *shiitake* mushrooms
1 pack *enoki* mushrooms or ½ pack champignons
1 oz snow peas
1 oz *harusame*
1 block tofu
3-in length *daikon* radish
Chili pepper
Broth:
6 cups stock (pp. 37–39)
¼ cup sakè
1 Tbsp soy sauce
1½ tsp salt
Dipping Sauce:
¼ cup lemon juice
¼ cup soy sauce
2 Tbsp water

1.   Devein and shell shrimp, leaving tail section intact. Gut squid and remove legs. Slice body into rings 1/2 in wide. Cut fish and shellfish into generous bite-size pieces. Wash Chinese cabbage or cabbage, cut in fairly large pieces, and boil briefly; it should still be crisp. Scrape carrot and cut into 1/4-in rounds. Slice white parts of scallions diagonally. Cut bamboo shoot into slices 1/4 in thick. Cut off and discard stems of *shiitake* mushrooms and wash under running water. Cut off and discard bases of *enoki* mushrooms. String snow peas. Dip *harusame* in boiling water till tender. Drain in colander and cool in cold water. Cut into convenient lengths. Wash tofu. Cut lengthwise in half then crosswise in slices 1/2 in thick. Arrange all ingredients attractively on serving plates.

Combine broth ingredients. Grate *daikon* radish, drain in a colander till it is about half its original weight, and flavor with a dash of chili pepper. Combine sauce ingredients in a pitcher or other serving vessel.

2.   Fill a large ceramic casserole about 70 percent full with broth. Over some portable heating unit, at the dining table, bring the broth to the boil. Gradually add some of the seafoods and vegetables and cook to the desired degree of doneness. The tofu takes about a minute. Do not overcook the *harusame*.

Each diner should be provided with an individual bowl in which to put the cooked ingredients of his choice. Lemon and soy sauce are used to season the ingredients, which are eaten with a garnish of grated *daikon* radish. The same individual bowl is used to drink the broth.

Note: Do not try cooking all the ingredients at once. Beginning with the fish—or chicken— which enrich the flavor of the broth, add a little of each kind at a time. None of these ingredients should be overcooked. Replenish broth as it is used up or boiled off. It may be necessary to go to a market specializing in oriental foods for some of the ingredients called for in this recipe.

Cod *Chirinabe* (*Serves 4*)

The broth in which this one-pot dinner is cooked is unseasoned; consequently, a dipping sauce is provided. It is said that *chirinabe* originated during the Edo period (1600–1867) in Nagasaki. During this phase of its history, Japan was isolated from the rest of the world, but a small group of Dutchmen was permitted to live in Nagasaki. Because these men disliked fish raw (sashimi), they had it cooked in small pots of hot water.

> **2 lbs cod fillet**
> **2 blocks tofu**
> **1 lb Chinese cabbage or cabbage**
> **1 pack *enoki* mushrooms or ½ pack champignons**
> **2 scallions**
> **1 carrot**
> **1 5-in square *kombu* or instant stock**
> **6 oz *daikon* radish**
> *Dipping Sauce:*
> **¼ cup lemon juice**
> **¼ cup soy sauce**

1. Wash and bone cod. Cut into generous bite-size (about 1 oz) pieces. Cut tofu into 6 equal cubes. Cut Chinese cabbage into fairly large pieces and boil briefly; it should still be crisp. Cut off and discard bases of *enoki* mushrooms or slice champignons. Slice scallions on the diagonal. Slice carrot into thin rounds.

Arrange all ingredients attractively on a large serving dish.

Wipe both sides of *kombu* with paper towels. Peel and grate *daikon* radish and drain in a colander. Combine sauce ingredients.

2. Spread *kombu* in the bottom of a large ceramic casserole; fill about 60 percent full of water. Over a portable heating unit, at the dining table, bring the water to the boil and immediately add cod and then, little by little, the other ingredients.

3. Each diner is provided with an individual bowl for dipping sauce and grated *daikon* radish with which to season the foods he selects for himself from the casserole.

Thin the liquor in the pot with water if it becomes too strong.

Udonsuki (*Serves 4*)

Made with *udon* noodles, seafood, chicken, and vegetables, this one-pot dish is lighter than the more famous and heftier *sukiyaki*.

> **4 packages boiled *udon* noodles**
> **½ lb boned chicken thigh meat**
> **1 lb white-flesh fish (cod, bass, sea bream, halibut, and so on)**
> **1 Tbsp soy sauce**

8 shrimp
4 oz canned bamboo shoots
8 leaves Chinese cabbage
1 carrot
1 oz snow peas
8 fresh *shiitake* **mushrooms**
8 slices *kamaboko*
Broth:
  6 cups stock (pp. 37–39)
  2 Tbsp sakè
  ½ tsp salt
  1 Tbsp soy sauce
Garnishes:
  Lemon or lime
  Shichimi **mixed pepper**
  5 chopped scallions

1. Cut chicken and cod in generous bite-size pieces and sprinkle with 1 Tbsp soy sauce. Devein and shell shrimp, leaving tail-section shell intact. Cut bamboo shoots in 1/4-in slices. Cut Chinese cabbage into fairly large pieces and parboil; it should still be crisp. Cut carrot into 1/4-in rounds and parboil. String snow peas. Cut off and discard stems of *shiitake* mushrooms. Wash. Arrange all of these ingredients together with *udon* noodles and *kamaboko* attractively on a large serving plate. Combine broth ingredients. Arrange garnishes in individual serving dishes.
2. Over a portable heating unit, at the table, fill a large ceramic casserole 70 percent full of broth and bring to a boil over a low heat. Little by little add noodles, chicken, fish, *kamaboko*, and vegetables. After about 3 minutes, diners may select the ingredients of their choices, put them in individual bowls, and season them with garnishes. The liquor remaining in the casserole is drunk as soup.

Note: Cook chicken, fish, and vegetables as they are needed, in small amounts. Have a reserve of broth on hand to add when necessary. It may be necessary to go to a market specializing in oriental foods for some of the ingredients required in this recipe.

Entrées

Chopped Bonito
(*Katsuo-no-tataki*) (p. 57)

Sashimi

In the seventeenth century, raw fish was firmed in vinegar before being eaten.
Later, however, people came to see that it is much more delicious eaten as it is
with a seasoning of soy sauce. Savoring different kinds of seafoods as they reach
the peak of their flavor in different seasons of the year is the source of a great deal
of culinary pleasure. The following make especially good sashimi: sea bream,
halibut, sole, sillago, bass, globe fish, Spanish mackerel, tuna, bonito, yellowtail,
mackerel, horse mackerel, sardines, carp, sweetfish, shrimp, abalone, turbo, squid,
blood clams, and scallops.

• *Preparing Sashimi at Home*

Although as prepared by the skilled *itamae-san* in a restaurant, sashimi seems
much too sophisticated and beautiful to reproduce domestically, there are easy
ways to make it in your own kitchen, where you may feel confident that it is fresh
and wholesome. Try to have at least one of the usual garnishes and provide
wasabi horseradish for piquancy.

Freshness is paramount. Since comparatively few Japanese men bring home
freshly caught fish, housewives generally rely on markets or fish dealers. Examine
the fish in the market yourself and ask the attendants whether it is suitable for
eating raw. In Japan, it is customary to sell sashimi fish cut into blocks that are
the right shape for further cutting and serving. Some stores sell sashimi in attractive packages complete with garnish and *wasabi*. Some fish for sashimi is sold
frozen; but in the cases of squid, shrimp, and shellfish, the live product is preferable.

Slicing the fish thin for serving too early can lead to spoilage and loss of flavor.
Consequently, avoid packaged sliced sashimi and select fish cut in blocks. Wash
the fish under running water, dry with paper towels, and allow to stand covered
with kitchen wrap. Slice immediately before serving.

● *Cutting*

Customarily a long, narrow-bladed (so-called willow-leaf) knife is used to slice sashimi, but an ordinary kitchen knife will do as long as it is sharp. To cut clean and even, hold the block of the fish in one hand and cut as you pull the blade toward you.

(1) *Hira-zukuri* (Straight Slicing)

Suitable for most kinds of fish, this is the basic procedure for slicing fillets of skinned fish.

1. Position the fish on the cutting board with the skin side up and the thickest part of the fillet away from you. Lightly grip the fish in the left hand and slice, slanting the knife slightly in the direction of your left hand. Slices should be of a thickness that is comfortable to eat in a bite.

2. Arrange the slices, overlapping on a diagonal, on the right edge of the cutting board.

(2) *Sogi-zukuri* (Diagonal Slicing)

This method is used when slices must be thin, as they are for *nigirizushi* (sushi prepared in small individual servings).

A. Place the fillet on the cutting board. Working from the left edge of the block and inclining the knife to the right, make slanting slices, cutting as you pull the knife toward you. Arrange the slices, overlapped, on the left edge of the cutting board.

B. Place the fillet on the cutting board. Working from the right edge and inclining the knife more than in the straight-slicing method, cut as you pull the blade toward you. This method is used to slice sea bream and other fishes very thin for a kind of sashimi called *arai*. The fish is refreshed by a bath in ice water before being eaten.

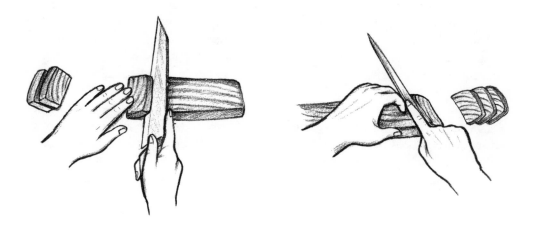

(3) *Kaku-zukuri* (Cubing)

This method, used for tender fish like tuna and bonito, is easy to employ at home.
1.   Slice the fillet lengthwise into suitable widths then cut it crosswise into cubes.
2.   Mound a few cubes on each serving plate and garnish with shredded *daikon* radish and grated *wasabi* horseradish.

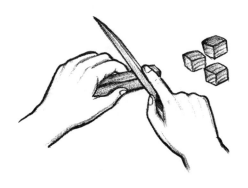

(4) *Ito-zukuri* (Julienne Cutting)

This method is used on squid and small fish like Spanish mackerel and sillago, with which cubing is impractical.
1.   Clean, skin, and fillet the fish. Using the point of the knife, cut the small fillets into julienne strips.
2.   Mound on individual serving plates and garnish with shredded *daikon* radish and grated *wasabi* horseradish.

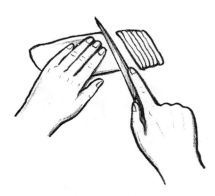

● *Garnishes for sashimi*

Employed to mask fishy odors and enhance flavors, garnishes are traditionally divided into three categories: *ken*, *tsuma*, and *karami*.

   1.   *Ken* or crisp garnishes.   These are usually shredded, crisp vegetables like *daikon* radish, Japanese-style cucumbers, or cabbage. They should be refreshed in cold water for from 10 to 20 minutes or dried, wrapped in kitchen wrap, and stored in the refrigerator for from 30 minutes to an hour. Arrange some of the vegetable of your choice on each individual serving plate and place the sashimi slices so as to rest on the garnish. Julienne-cut celery or iceberg lettuce too makes an acceptable crisp garnish.

2. *Tsuma* **or aromatic garnishes.** Placed on top of the sashimi, garnishes of this kind include the green leaves, buds, or sprouts of the *shiso* plant. *Shiso* leaves are often spread under sashimi.

3. *Karami* **or piquant garnish.** The most popular piquant garnish is *wasabi* horseradish. Commercially available *wasabi* powder must be mixed to a paste with water well in advance of serving time to allow full flavor to develop. Place a small mound of it before the sashimi in the serving dish. Fresh-ground *wasabi* is greatly superior. Using a fine grater, moving the root in a circular motion, and working from the end from which the leaves grew, grate the *wasabi* to a paste. If the root is too dry to grate, crush it with the back of a kitchen knife. Leftover *wasabi* may be wrapped in kitchen wrap and frozen.

The diner mixes the *wasabi* with soy sauce in a small dish provided for the purpose and dips the sashimi in the mixture before eating it.

• *Serving*

Place crisp vegetable garnish in the center of each individual serving dish. On top of this overlap 5 or 7 slices of sashimi. In front of these arrange another 3 slices. In Japan, it is considered a good idea to use uneven numbers of slices; but you need not feel constrained to respect this preference.

Nori-wrapped Tuna *(Serves 4)*

½ lb tuna
3 Asakusa *nori* sheets
Watercress
***Wasabi* horseradish**
Soy sauce

1. Cut tuna into strips about 2/3-in square. Wipe dry with paper towels.
2. Lightly toast *nori* sheets to heighten aroma. Cut each sheet in half parallel with the shorter sides. Spread a sheet of *nori* on a flat working surface, long side toward you. Place a strip of tuna in the center. Roll the *nori* around the tuna, beginning at the side closer to you. Cut off 2/3 in from one end. Arrange, cut end up, on a serving dish and garnish with watercress and *wasabi* horseradish. (Powdered *wasabi* must be mixed with water and allowed to stand a while for full flavor to develop.)

In small dipping dishes, combine soy sauce and *wasabi*. Diners dip *nori*-wrapped tuna in this seasoning before eating.

Chopped Bonito (*Katsuo-no-tataki*) *(Serves 4)*

This is a slightly simplified version of a famous regional specialty. Very fresh bonito fillet is skewered and quickly seared over a direct fire. In the traditional method, after a bath in cold water, it is lightly chopped together with seasonings.

1 lb fresh bonito
1 Tbsp salad oil
Salt
½ lb *daikon* radish
10 scallions, both green and white parts, chopped
1 Tbsp grated fresh ginger root
1 tsp crushed garlic
Lemon soy sauce (p. 30)

1. Skin the bonito, working from the head.
2. In a frying pan, heat 1 Tbsp salad oil. Have a bowl of ice water ready. Sear the fish 30 seconds to a side or about a minute and 30 seconds in all. Immediately plunge it in ice water. Dry with paper towels. Cut into slices 1/3 in thick. Arrange the slices, cut edges up, in a flat container. Sprinkle with salt.
3. Grate *daikon* radish and drain until reduced to about half original volume. Combine scallions, *daikon*, ginger root, and garlic. Sprinkle them evenly over the fish. Refrigerate for 30 minutes.
4. Arrange the fish and vegetables on a serving plate. Serve with a sauce made of equal parts of lemon juice and soy sauce.

Sautéed Dishes

Yellowtail Tahini
(p. 59)

Salmon Steak in Red-wine Sauce *(Serves 4)*

Salmon and red wine go together very well. This easily prepared dish is good for the bones and the blood since salmon is rich in both vitamin D and in vitamin B$_6$, which helps combat anemia.

> **4 salmon steaks (1 lb in all)**
> **Salt**
> **Pepper**
> **2 Tbsp vegetable oil**
> **½ cup dry red wine**
> **1 Tbsp butter**
> *Garnish:*
> **1 cucumber**
> **Salt**
> **3 scallions (white parts)**
> **Ginger root**

1. Dry salmon steaks with paper towels and sprinkle with salt and pepper. Heat vegetable oil in a frying pan and brown steaks on both sides.
2. Heat red wine in a saucepan; ignite to burn off alcohol. Simmer to reduce to 1/2 original volume. Add 2 Tbsp butter, stirring constantly. Season with salt and pepper.
3. Slice cucumbers about 1/4 in thick. Parboil in lightly salted water. Plunge at once into cold water. Julienne cut white part of scallions. Peel and julienne cut ginger root. Allow to stand in cold water for 20 minutes. Drain.
4. Arrange salmon on a serving plate. Decorate with cucumbers, coat with red-wine sauce, and garnish with ginger, scallions, and boiled potatoes (see below).

Potato Preparation

Peel potatoes and cut in half. Boil till tender. Pour off liquid. Shaking the unlidded pan gently, dry the potatoes over a moderate heat. Season with salt and pepper.

Yellowtail Tahini *(Serves 4)*

Sesame seeds, the base of tahini paste, are highly recommended for people concerned about blood-cholesterol levels. Tahini paste is easy to digest and greatly enhances the aroma of seafood dishes. It is sold bottled in Middle Eastern food markets. You may substitute butterfish, swordfish, mackerel, or bonito for yellowtail.

4 yellowtail fillets (1 lb in all)
2 Tbsp tahini paste
2 Tbsp soy sauce
2 Tbsp sakè or sherry
$\frac{1}{2}$ Tbsp sesame oil
$\frac{1}{2}$ Tbsp juice from grated, fresh ginger
$\frac{1}{2}$ tsp crushed garlic
4 scallions (white part)
***Daikon*-radish sprouts or alfalfa sprouts**
4 Tbsp flour
2 Tbsp salad oil

1. Remove any bones that may remain in the fillets. With a wire whip, soften the tahini paste in a small bowl. Add soy sauce, sakè, sesame oil, ginger juice, and garlic. Mix well. Marinate fish in this mixture for 2 hours.
2. Julienne cut the white part of the scallions and soak in cold water for from 20 to 30 minutes. Drain well and refrigerate. Remove and discard roots of *daikon*-radish sprouts. Cut in half, wash, and drain.
3. Scrape marinade from fillets and flour them.
4. Heat salad oil in a frying pan. Brown fillets on both sides.
5. Arrange fillets on a serving plate. Top with scallion and *daikon*-radish sprouts (or alfalfa).

Mackerel in Sour-cream Sauce *(Serves 4)*

Sour cream is a delicious accompaniment to fish. You may substitute Spanish mackerel, sardine, bass, bonito, butterfish, cod, halibut, horse mackerel, orange roughy, sea bream, sole, or swordfish for mackerel.

1 large mackerel, $1\frac{1}{2}$ lbs
Salt
Pepper
Cayenne pepper
2 Tbsp butter
$\frac{1}{2}$ cup milk
1 tsp Dijon mustard
$\frac{1}{4}$ cup chopped scallions
$\frac{1}{4}$ cup sour cream
Watercress

1. Clean and fillet mackerel. Cut the two fillets into 8 pieces.
2. Sprinkle fish with salt and allow it to stand for 20 minutes. Wash and dry with paper towels. Sprinkle with pepper and cayenne pepper.
3. In a frying pan heat butter. Add fillets. Cover pan and sauté for from 3 to 5 minutes a side, or until brown.
4. Remove from heat. Combine milk and mustard and pour over fish. Without a lid, simmer until fish is done and volume of milk has been reduced. Season to taste. Sprinkle fish with chopped scallions. Add sour cream and blend well.
5. Arrange fillets on a serving dish, top with the sauce from the frying pan, and garnish with watercress.

Salmon and Tofu *(Serves 4)*

Tofu sandwiched between slices of salmon is fried for a healthful main dish. You may substitute bass, halibut, mackerel, or horse mackerel for salmon.

> **4 salmon fillets ($\frac{3}{4}$ lb in all)**
> **$\frac{1}{2}$ block (7 oz) tofu**
> **Salt**
> **1 Tbsp sakè or sherry**
> **3 oz small shelled shrimp**
> **1 Tbsp salad oil**
> **$\frac{1}{2}$ egg**
> **$\frac{1}{4}$ tsp salt**
> **Leaf lettuce**
> **Radishes**
> **Lemon**

1. Place the tofu in a saucepan full of cold water. Bring to a boil and simmer for 30 seconds. Drain in a colander. Use an egg beater to crumble tofu coarse. Refrigerate for from 1 to 2 hours. Drain. Before frying, drain again on paper towels.
2. Cut salmon into 8 thin slices 3 by 2 in. Sprinkle with salt and sakè and allow to stand for 10 minutes.
3. Chop shelled shrimp. Sauté in salad oil. Lightly beat egg. Combine egg, shrimp, tofu, and 1/4 tsp salt. Divide into 4 equal parts.
4. Dry salmon slices with paper towels. Place a quarter of the tofu mixture on top of each of 4 salmon slices; top each with one of the remaining salmon slices.
5. In a frying pan, heat 2 tsp salad oil over a medium heat. Fry salmon-tofu sandwiches 3 minutes on a side, turn and fry another 4 minutes. Cover pan and cook till done.
6. Arrange washed leaf lettuce in a circle in the center of a serving plate and sprinkle with sliced radishes. Place salmon-tofu sandwiches in the center and decorate each with a slice of lemon.

Fragrant Fried Yellowtail *(Serves 4)*

Use half again as much sakè if you intend to marinate the fish overnight. You
may substitute mackerel, salmon, bonito, horse mackerel, or swordfish for yellowtail.

> **4 yellowtail fillets (1 lb in all)**
> **¹⁄₂ onion**
> **¹⁄₄ cup flour**
> **2 Tbsp salad oil**
> **Watercress**
> *Marinade:*
> **2 Tbsp soy sauce**
> **2 Tbsp sakè or sherry**
> **1 tsp sesame oil**
> **1 tsp juice from grated fresh ginger**
> **1 tsp crushed garlic**

1. Combine marinade ingredients and marinate fish for 2 hours. Slice onion thin
and allow to stand in cold water for 10 minutes. Wrap in paper towels and
squeeze dry.
2. Drain fish and coat with flour.
3. In a frying pan, heat salad oil. Fry fish till brown. Arrange fish on a serving
plate, surround with sliced onion, and garnish with watercress.

Swordfish in Ginger-garlic Sauce *(Serves 4)*

You may substitute tuna, Spanish mackerel, bonito, salmon, mackerel, horse
mackerel, or shark for the swordfish.

> **4 swordfish steaks (1 lb in all)**
> **²⁄₃ tsp salt**
> **Pepper**
> **4 Tbsp flour**
> **4 Tbsp salad oil**
> **Juice of 1 lemon**
> **1 Tbsp sesame oil**
> **1 Tbsp crushed fresh ginger**
> **1 Tbsp crushed garlic**
> **4 scallions, chopped**
> **Chili pepper (optional)**

1. Sprinkle swordfish steaks with salt and pepper and allow to stand for 20
minutes.
2. Dry with paper towels and coat with flour. In a frying pan heat 2 Tbsp salad

oil. Brown fish on both sides. Remove to a serving plate and sprinkle with lemon juice. Discard remaining oil in frying pan.

3. Combine 2 Tbsp salad oil and sesame oil in frying pan. Add ginger and garlic and sauté for about 10 seconds, taking care not to scorch. Remove from heat and add scallions and chili pepper if desired. Top swordfish steaks with this sauce.

Tuna Meunière with Cheese *(Serves 4)*

Low in oil, tuna is good for both health and appearance. Furthermore, it helps prevent anemia because it is rich in A and B vitamin groups and in iron. The melted cheese topping is a delicious addition. You may substitute such firm-fleshed fish as swordfish, bonito, and salmon for the tuna.

> **4 tuna steaks (1 lb in all)**
> **Salt**
> **Pepper**
> **¼ cup lemon juice**
> **Flour**
> **Salad oil**
> **¼ cup chopped scallion**
> **4 oz cheese**
> *Garnish:*
> **2 potatoes**
> **2 tomatoes**
> **Salad oil**
> **Salt**
> **Pepper**
> **Watercress**

1. Sprinkle tuna steaks with salt, pepper, and lemon juice and allow to stand for 5 minutes.
2. Dry with paper towels and flour. In a frying pan, heat salad oil. Brown tuna steaks on both sides. Sprinkle chopped scallions on fish and grate cheese on top. Cover with a lid and simmer over a medium heat until fish is done and cheese has melted.
3. Place tuna steaks in the front of a serving plate. Behind them arrange, in alternation, potato and tomato garnish prepared as explained below. Place watercress on tuna steaks.

Garnish

Peel potatoes and cut into rounds 1/3 in thick. Boil gently, taking care not to allow them to crumble. Cut tomatoes in similar rounds. Heat salad oil in a frying pan. Sprinkle both sides of potato and tomato slices with salt and pepper. Fry tomato briefly. Fry potato till golden brown.

Yellowtail *Teriyaki* (Serves 4)

This simple *teriyaki* is cooked in a frying pan. If *mirin* is unavailable, substitute sakè sweetened with a tsp sugar. If you have plenty of time, the fish may be marinated for as long as half a day. You may substitute mackerel, Spanish mackerel, swordfish, sea bream, or butterfish for the yellowtail.

> **4 yellowtail fillets (1 lb in all)**
> **Flour**
> **2 Tbsp salad oil**
> **8 radishes**
> *Marinade:*
> **2 Tbsp soy sauce**
> **¼ cup sakè or sherry**
> **1 Tbsp *mirin* (sweetened sakè)**

1. Combine marinade ingredients. Marinate yellowtail for 30 minutes, turning from time to time.
2. Dry fish steaks and coat with flour.
3. Heat salad oil in a frying pan. Fry fish till golden brown on one side. Turn and fry till almost done. Pour off oil. Add remaining marinade to fish in pan. Cover pan and cook till fish is done.
4. Remove lid and, shaking pan gently all the while, continue to cook until most of the liquid has evaporated. Arrange on serving plate and top with remaining sauce. Garnish with radish roses cut as shown below and allowed to stand in cold water for an hour.

Sautéed Oysters in Ketchup Sauce (Serves 4)

The subtle blend of oyster and ketchup flavors is very pleasing. Since the oysters are parboiled first, the sautéing must be very quick.

> **¾ lb oysters (medium)**
> **4 ginger slices**
> **3 scallions (cut in 3-in lengths)**
> **1 egg**
> **½ Tbsp soy sauce**
> **1 Tbsp sakè**

$\frac{1}{2}$ Tbsp juice from grated fresh ginger
$\frac{1}{4}$ cup cornstarch
$\frac{1}{4}$ cup flour
3 Tbsp salad oil
1 Tbsp sesame oil
3 scallions (white part), chopped
Broccoli
Steamed rice
Sauce:
$1\frac{1}{2}$ Tbsp soy sauce
3 Tbsp ketchup
4 Tbsp chicken stock
1 tsp cornstarch

1.   In a saucepan combine a small amount of boiling water, ginger, and scallions. Add oysters and boil briefly. Drain in a colander. Discard ginger and scallion. (The liquor may be reserved for use in miso soup.)
2.   Lightly beat egg and combine with soy sauce, sakè, and ginger. Marinate oysters in mixture for 20 minutes.
3.   Combine cornstarch and flour and add to oyster mixture.
4.   Heat salad oil in a frying pan. Fry oysters, turning as necessary. (Cook in batches suited to the size of the frying pan.) Remove oysters and set aside.
5.   Combine sauce ingredients and add to frying pan. Heat, stirring constantly. Add oysters to sauce and stir till they are coated. Add sesame oil.
6.   Heap oysters on a serving plate. Sprinkle with chopped scallions. Serve with boiled broccoli and steamed rice.

Squid in Oriental Sauce *(Serves 4)*

This is a very easy and delicious dish. Squid is sautéed in salad oil and seasoned with oriental sauce. Cut the squid thick. Its high taurin content helps prevent such illnesses as cardiac infarction.

4 slices fresh or frozen squid (each weighing $\frac{1}{3}$ lb)
Salt
Pepper
$\frac{1}{4}$ cup white wine
$\frac{1}{4}$ cup and 2 Tbsp salad oil
1 tsp crushed garlic
1 stalk celery
Shredded curly endive
1 carrot, diced and boiled
Dressing:
3 Tbsp lemon juice
2 tsp soy sauce
2 Tbsp salad oil

1 tsp juice from grated fresh ginger
Pepper

1. Fresh squid must be cleaned: internal organs, tentacles, and thin outer skin must be removed and discarded. Frozen squid has been cleaned and needs only to be thawed. Cut squid in fairly large bite-size pieces. Sprinkle with salt and pepper. Combine white wine, 1/4 cup salad oil, and garlic and marinate squid in them for 20 minutes. Dry on paper towels.
2. Slice celery diagonally and lightly sauté in 1 Tbsp hot salad oil. Set aside.
3. In a frying pan, heat 1 Tbsp salad oil. Sauté squid in oil on both sides briefly. Overexposure to heat toughens it. Fry only till the color has changed.
4. With a wire whip or rotary egg beater combine dressing ingredients in a small bowl. Divide the dressing among 4 individual serving dishes. Place some squid in the center of each. Top squid with sautéed celery. Arrange shredded endive around the edge of the plate and sprinkle with boiled diced carrot.

Fried Foods

Fried Bass and Eggplant
in Tomato Sauce (p. 74)

● *Hints for Perfect Tempura*

Tempura is the name given to foods coated in batter and quickly fried in plenty of
hot oil. Heat evaporates some of the moisture in the ingredients, whose flavors
blend appetizingly with the fragrance of the oil. Other frying methods involve no
batter. Sometimes such food as eggplant or sliced sweet potatoes are fried with no
coating at all. Shrimp and seafood may be breaded or simply coated in flour or
cornstarch for frying.

● *Oils*

Use vegetable oils—corn, peanut, soy, sesame, olive, and so on. Corn and peanut
oils are preferred, though they may be made more interesting with additions of
other kinds.

● *Equipment*

Pans: Use a deep, heavy frying pan. The Chinese wok is convenient because it
permits ample frying space with a minimum amount of oil.

Convenient Layout for Frying Tempura

Long chopsticks or tongs: For lifting foods into and out of hot oil.

Wire rack and shallow pan: For draining fried foods. Do not layer fried foods for draining, since oil dripping down from above makes the bottom layer soggy.

Paper towels: For draining fried foods when rack and pan are unavailable.

Mesh scoop: For removing extraneous bits of fried batter, which burn and spoil oil.

● *Oil Quantities*

The ingredients should be able to float free in the hot oil. But, since disposing of large quantities after cooking is a problem, enough oil to cover is sufficient.

● *Batter*

To ensure light, crisp batter, chill flour and egg and use chilled (ice) water. Lightly beat egg, add 1 cup flour, then add cold water all at once. Blend rapidly with a fork. Ignore small lumps.

Measure 1 cup flour and 1 cup ice water.

Sift flour.

In a chilled bowl, combine 1 egg and 1 cup ice water. Mix well.

Add 1 cup sifted flour and mix lightly and swiftly with fork or egg beater.

● *Oil Temperatures*

This varies somewhat with ingredients, but in general, between 300° and 350°F is good.

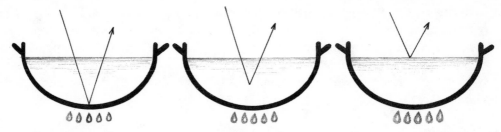

300°–310°F	320°–350°F	400°F
A drop of batter sinks to the bottom of the pan and then floats to the surface. This temperature is good for slow-cooking ingredients. During the last few minutes, raise the temperature to crisp the batter.	A drop of batter sinks halfway to the bottom of the pan and then floats to the surface at once. This is the right temperature for most tempura.	Without sinking at all, a drop of batter remains dancing about on the surface of the oil, which is so hot that it burns ingredients before they are done through.

Words of caution about frying

Never leave a pan of hot oil unattended on a heat source. If the telephone or something else compels you to be away for a moment, always turn the heat off. If the oil should happen to ignite, lower its temperature by adding green leafy vegetables to the pan. Cover with thick cloth to shut out air.

Disposing of oil after frying

While it is still warm, strain oil through a coffee filter or paper towels. Cool. Cover with a lid or kitchen wrap and store in a cool, dark place. It may be used, little by little, for sautés or for cooking such things as hamburgers. Add fresh oil before using it again for tempura.

Ginger juice in batter

To ensure light, crisp tempura, professionals add a few drops of ginger juice to the batter. An enzyme in ginger is said to break down gluten and prevent the batter from toughening. Moreover, the fragrance of ginger helps mask fishy odors.

Mixed Tempura *(Serves 4)*

Seafood tempura is highly appetizing. The frying process masks fish odors. Do not feel limited to the ingredients listed below. Use whatever you have in your refrigerator.

> ¾ lb halibut or other white-flesh fish
> 8 shrimp
> 5 oz acorn squash
> 1 onion

    8 asparagus
    2 green peppers
    Salt
    Pepper
    Capers
    Mayonnaise
    Oil for frying (corn or peanut oil)
    Flour
    Celery salt
    Lemon wedges
  Batter:
    1 egg and chilled water to make 1 cup
    1 cup sifted flour
    $\frac{1}{2}$ tsp baking powder

1.   Slice halibut 1/3 in thick then into bite-size pieces. Leaving the tail shell intact, shell and devein shrimp (pp. 132–133). Make 3 or 4 incisions in the belly side to prevent curling during frying. Cut acorn squash into slices 1/4 in thick and 2 by 1 in. Cut onion into 8 equal wedges and skewer with bamboo skewers to prevent sections from separating. Snap off hard, lower parts of asparagus stalks. Cut asparagus in half. Seed green peppers and cut into rings 1/3 in thick.

2.   In chilled bowl, lightly beat egg. Add chilled water to make 1 cup. Add flour and baking powder all at once. Mix briefly with a fork. Ignore small lumps. Prepare a shallow bowl of flour in which to coat ingredients before they are dipped into batter (see p. 66 for suggested layout).

3.   Combine salt, pepper, capers, and mayonnaise.

4.   In a deep frying pan or a wok, heat oil to 350°F.

5.   With long chopsticks or tongs dip pieces of halibut first in flour then in batter. Fry till the surface of the batter is crisp. Drain on a rack. Lifting them in the fingers by the tail shell, dip shrimp first in flour and then in batter. Since they cook quickly, a minute or 2 in the hot oil is enough. Repeat the same process with the acorn squash and asparagus. They are done when a fork pierces them with little resistance. Repeat the process with the onions. Dry the green peppers and fry briefly without coating with either flour or batter. Drain all fried ingredients on a wire rack or on paper towels.

5.   Arrange tempura on a large serving dish spread with paper napkins. Sprinkle with celery salt, garnish with lemon wedges, and serve with the flavored mayonnaise.

Frying Shrimp
Even if the amount of shrimp to be fried is small, use plenty of oil. Heat oil to the temperature suited to the ingredients. At no time should the food being fried cover more than 3/4 of the surface of the oil. Maintain a constant temperature.

Drop a small amount of the batter gently into the oil. If it sinks halfway to the bottom of the pan and then rises again the temperature is between 325° and 350°F, or just right for seafood tempura.

Holding a shrimp by the tail shell, dip it first in flour.

Then dip it in batter. A generous coating of batter is desirable.

Next quickly drop the shrimp into the center of the boil. Add a few more.

As they cook, turn the shrimp with long chopsticks or tongs to ensure doneness and an evenly crisp outer crust.

When a shrimp is done, lift it from the oil. Shake it lightly to remove as much oil as possible. Drain on a rack in a flat pan. Do not overlap fried tempura.

Breaded Fried Salmon with Almonds *(Serves 4)*

Like seafood, nuts are rich in a kind of oil that prevents arteriosclerosis. The two therefore make an excellent and delicious combination. You may substitute walnuts, peanuts, or pecans for the almonds. Any fillet fish may be substituted for the salmon.

> 4 salmon fillets ($\frac{3}{4}$ lb in all)
> Salt
> Pepper
> 1 stalk celery
> 2 green sweet peppers
> 2 red sweet peppers
> 1 egg
> $\frac{1}{2}$ tsp salad oil
> $\frac{1}{2}$ tsp water
> $\frac{1}{2}$ cup crushed almonds
> 1 cup bread crumbs
> Flour
> Oil for frying
> Lemon wedges

1. Skin the salmon and remove any persisting bones. Cut into 20 bite-size pieces. Season with salt and pepper. Scrape celery and cut it into 4-in julienne strips. Seed peppers and cut into rings 1/3 in thick.
2. Lightly beat egg and combine with salad oil and water. Mix well.
3. Mix crushed almonds (if they are whole, they may be crushed in a blender or enclosed in kitchen wrap and crushed with a rolling pin) with bread crumbs.
4. Flour salmon and celery, dip in egg mixture, and roll in bread crumbs and crushed almonds. (It is a good idea to complete the recipe to this step several hours before frying time.)
5. Heat oil to 325° F. Fry salmon and celery to golden brown. Take care not to allow the oil to become hot enough to burn the ingredients. Fry the peppers in the oil with no coating of any kind.
6. Arrange in a serving dish spread with paper napkins or a paper lace doily, sprinkle with salt and pepper, and serve garnished with lemon wedges.

Salmon Two-tone Fry *(Serves 4)*

> $\frac{3}{4}$ lb salmon
> Salt
> Pepper
> 2 Tbsp flour
> 2 Tbsp chopped parsley
> 2 Tbsp chopped celery leaves
> 1 each red and green sweet peppers
> Peppers
> Oil for frying
> Lemon wedges

Coating:
    1 egg and ice water to make 1 cup
    1 cup flour

1. Cut salmon into bite-size pieces and season with salt and pepper.
2. Dredge salmon in flour, taking care to shake off excess.
3. Beat egg lightly and combine with ice water. Add flour and stir with a fork. Divide into 2 equal batches. To 1 batch add chopped parsley; add chopped celery leaves to other batch.
4. Slice peppers into strips 1/2 in wide and dry thoroughly.
5. In a deep frying pan, heat oil to 350°F. Dip half of salmon pieces in 1 of the coating mixtures and fry till golden brown. Drain on paper towels. Repeat with remaining salmon pieces dipped into other coating mixture. Briefly fry pepper strips, without coating, and drain. Season with salt.
6. Arrange salmon pieces on a serving dish. Garnish with peppers and lemon wedges.

Salmon *Nambu* Fry *(Serves 4)*

Nambu, a district in the northeastern part of the main Japanese island of Honshu, gives its name to various kinds of foods incorporating sesame seeds. In this fragrant dish, sesame seeds are included in the tempura-style batter in which the fish is dipped before frying. Virtually any kind of fish fillet may be substituted for the salmon.

    4 salmon fillets (1 lb in all)
    ⅔ tsp salt
    Pepper
    1 stalk celery
    8 pods okra
    Oil for frying
    Lemon wedges
Batter:
    1 cup flour
    1 egg and chilled water to make 1 cup
    2 Tbsp white sesame seeds

1. Cut salmon fillets in half, season with salt and pepper, and allow to stand 20 minutes.
2. Scrape celery and cut into 2-in lengths. Slit wide parts for easy eating. Wash okra.
3. Using a fork, combine batter ingredients. Ignore small lumps.
4. Heat oil to 325° F.
5. Dry fish with paper towels. Coat in batter and fry for from 5 to 6 minutes in oil. Remove to rack and drain.

6.   Coat celery in batter and fry for from 3 to 4 minutes, or until crisp. Remove to rack and drain. Coat okra with batter and repeat the same process.

7.   Combine salmon, celery, and okra in a large serving dish; sprinkle with salt and pepper; and serve garnished with lemon wedges.

Fried Pacific Butterfish *(Serves 4)*

The fish, fried whole, is served with a dressing flavored with soy sauce and accompanied with hot steamed rice. You may substitute horse mackerel, sea bream, or turbot for Pacific butterfish.

> **2 Pacific butterfish (1 lb each)**
> **2 Tbsp sakè**
> **1 Tbsp soy sauce**
> **1 tsp ginger juice**
> **Oil for frying**
> *Sauce:*
> **4 scallions (white part), chopped**
> **$\frac{1}{2}$ Tbsp soy sauce**
> **1 tsp sakè**

1.   Clean butterfish (p. 130).

2.   With the head on the left and the belly side forward, make 2 deep incisions in the flesh. Incline knife to one side and cut all the way to the spine.

3.   Combine sakè, soy sauce, and ginger juice. Allow fish to marinate in this mixture for 30 minutes. Spoon liquid over fish occasionally.

4.   Heat oil to 350° F. Dry fish and fry for about 10 minutes, ladling hot oil over it from time to time.

5.   Combine sauce ingredients. Arrange fried butterfish on a serving platter and top with this sauce.

Fried Turbot *(Serves 4)*

The simple method of coating with only flour or cornstarch before frying makes the most of delicate seafood flavors. You may substitute practically any fish for turbot, though, if large, it should be filleted.

> **4 turbot (medium)**
> **8 stalks green asparagus**
> **Oil for frying**
> **Flour**
> **Salt**
> **Pepper**
> **1 Tbsp lemon juice**
> **1 Tbsp soy sauce**

1. Scale and clean turbot (see p. 130). Wash thoroughly and make long crosswise incisions in the central part of the upper (dark) side. Dry well with paper towels.
2. Discard hard lower parts of asparagus and cut stalks in half.
3. Heat oil to 325° F.
4. Dust fish with flour, patting to remove excess. Fry slowly, dark side up. In the last few minutes, raise oil temperature to 350° F to crisp fish.
5. With no coating at all, fry asparagus for a few minutes. Sprinkle with salt and pepper.
6. Arrange fish, dark side up, on a serving platter and garnish with asparagus. Season with salt or serve with a dressing of half and half lemon juice and soy sauce.

Note: Use plenty of oil. Coat the entire fish quickly with flour and pat off excess. Since moisture in the fish may make the oil spatter, use a fairly large pan. If you use a lid, crack it slightly to allow steam to escape. It may be necessary to ladle hot oil over parts of the fish that refuse to remain submerged. You may substitute some other fried vegetable for asparagus.

Curry-flavored Mackerel Fry *(Serves 4)*

> ¾ lb mackerel fillets
> 3 Tbsp cornstarch
> 2 tsp curry powder
> Oil for frying
> Leaf lettuce

1. Cut mackerel into bite-size pieces about 1/5 in thick. Salt and allow to stand for 20 minutes. Dry with paper towels.
2. Mix cornstarch and curry powder. Dredge mackerel pieces with this mixture, taking care to shake off excess.
3. In a deep frying pan, heat oil to 325°F. Fry mackerel pieces for about 2 minutes, or until golden.
4. Serve on a bed of lettuce torn into bite-size pieces.

Fried Bass and Eggplant in Tomato Sauce *(Serves 6)*

An Italian-style dish featuring fried bass and eggplant broiled in tomato sauce with a mozzarella-cheese topping.

> 1 lb sliced bass
> Salt
> Pepper
> ¼ cup white wine
> Oil (preferably corn oil) for frying
> Cornstarch
> 2 small Japanese-style eggplant (4 oz each)

½ cup tomato sauce
½ cup grated mozzarella cheese
Lemon slices

1.   Salt and pepper bass slices (about 1/4 in thick), sprinkle with white wine, and allow to stand for 20 minutes.
2.   In a deep frying pan or wok, heat to 350° F just enough oil to cover fish slices. Dry fish with paper towels. Coat lightly and evenly with cornstarch. Fry in oil for about 2 minutes, or until golden brown. Turn once during the frying. Drain on paper towels.
3.   Wash eggplant and remove and discard stalks and calyxes. Cut diagonally into slices 1/4 in thick. Coat with cornstarch and fry at 350° F for 2 minutes. Turn once during frying. Drain on paper towels. Sprinkle with salt and pepper.
4.   Arrange eggplant slices in an ovenproof dish, coat with tomato sauce. Add fish and top with grated cheese. Broil until cheese is melted. Serve garnished with lemon slices.

Note: You may substitute halibut, cod, red snapper, or salmon for the bass. If the slices of fish and eggplant are small, this dish makes an attractive hors d'oeuvre.

Red Sea Bream, Fried Then Steamed *(Serves 4)*

In Japan, the red sea bream, or *tai*, is traditionally served on festive occasions like weddings. Recently, imported shrimp too have been finding a place in such festivities, but it is wise to remember the old saying that shrimp are used as bait to catch sea bream. In other words, it is possible to use something small and insignificant, like a shrimp, to obtain great reward, like a sea bream. In this recipe, the sea bream is first fried in a small amount of oil and then steamed with an aromatic topping. You may substitute bass, bonito, or horse mackerel for sea bream.

   1 (2 lb) red sea bream (or fillets 1 lb)
   ½ tsp salt
   Pepper
   6 scallions (white part)
   ⅓ cup salad oil
   8 cilantro leaves
Seasoning:
   3 cloves crushed garlic
   5 slices ginger root
   1 red chili pepper (seeded)
   ½ cup sakè
   1½ Tbsp soy sauce

1.   Scale and clean sea bream (see p. 130). Wash thoroughly. Dry well. Sprinkle

inside and out with salt and pepper and allow to stand for 20 minutes. If fillets are being used, salt and pepper them in the same way.

2. Cut scallions into 1/2-in lengths. Divide each section vertically into quarters. Heat salad oil in a large frying pan. Dry fish carefully and brown on one side over a medium-to-strong heat for 5 minutes. Turn, lower heat, and cook 4 minutes longer. Remove from pan and drain. Discard oil remaining in pan.

3. Combine seasoning ingredients. Return fish to pan. Pour seasoning over it, cover with a lid, and steam over a low heat for 3 minutes.

4. Sprinkle fish with scallions, cover, and steam an additional minute. Remove and discard garlic and ginger.

5. Arrange fish on a serving platter, top with sauce from pan, and surround with a border of cilantro leaves.

Shrimp in Kiwi-fruit Sauce *(Serves 4)*

The attractive combination of pink shrimp and green kiwi-fruit sauce plus aromatic cashew nuts makes for very appetizing dining.

> $1\frac{1}{2}$ lb shrimp (medium or large)
> $\frac{1}{3}$ cup white wine
> **Salt**
> **1 egg white**
> **1 Tbsp cornstarch**
> **2 kiwi fruit (for garnish)**
> **Oil for frying (corn or peanut)**
> $\frac{1}{2}$ cup unsalted cashew nuts
> **Curly lettuce**
> *Kiwi-fruit Sauce:*
> **2 kiwi fruit**
> **1 Tbsp white wine**

1. Shell and devein shrimp. Combine white wine and salt and marinate shrimp in mixture for 20 minutes.

2. Dry shrimp with paper towels. In a bowl, lightly beat egg white. Add shrimp then cornstarch and mix well.

3. Peel 2 kiwi fruit. Cut out and discard parts containing black seeds. Force remaining pulp through a sieve or strainer with the back of a tablespoon. Blend sieved pulp with white wine to make sauce. Peel and slice remaining kiwi fruit.

4. Heat oil to 325° F. Fry shrimp till color changes. Drain. In the same oil, fry cashew nuts till golden brown. Drain and chop.

5. In the center of each serving plate, pour a little kiwi-fruit sauce. Place a leaf of curly lettuce in the sauce. Top the leaf with some of the fried shrimp. Garnish with slices of kiwi fruit and sprinkle with fried, chopped cashew nuts.

Squid Tempura and Squid Fritters *(Serves 4)*

For success with this kind of tempura, remember to score the squid flesh with a sharp knife at 1/4-in intervals. Since squid has a high moisture content, beware of spattering hot oil.

> ¹⁄₂ **lb cleaned squid**
> **Oil for frying (corn or peanut)**
> **Flour**
> **Salt**
> **Lemon wedges**
> *Batter:*
> **1 egg and chilled water to make ³⁄₄ cup**
> ³⁄₄ **cup flour**
> *Squid Fritter:*
> ¹⁄₂ **cup squid tentacles (cut to ¹⁄₃-in lengths)**
> **1 cup sliced celery**
> **2 Tbsp flour**
> *Fritter Batter:*
> ¹⁄₂ **cup flour**
> ¹⁄₂ **egg and chilled water to make ¹⁄₂ cup**

● *Tempura*

1.   Score squid meat at 1/4-in intervals. Turn and score again to make a diagonal checkerboard pattern. Cut into pieces about 1 1/2 by 2/3 in.

2.   In a chilled bowl lightly beat egg. Add chilled water and the flour, all at once. Beat with a fork, lightly and briefly. Ignore small lumps.

3.   Heat oil to 350° F.

4.   Coat squid slices first in flour then in batter. Fry till batter is crisp. Drain on wire rack or paper towels. The tempura will drain better if stood on edge.

5.   Line a serving plate with paper napkins. Arrange tempura on it. Sprinkle with salt and serve with lemon wedges.

After removing the thin outer skin, score the squid with diagonal incisions made at an interval of 1/4 in.

Turn the squid and score again to make a diagonal checkerboard pattern that enables flour and batter to cling better and helps prevent oil from spattering.

Cut into suitable slices.

● *Squid Fritters*
1. Drain cut squid tentacles in a colander.
2. Combine ingredients listed under fritter batter in the same way as those for tempura batter.
3. Heat oil to 350° F.

Add 1/2 cup chilled water to lightly beaten egg. Sift 1/2 cup flour.

Preliminary preparations.

Pour water and egg into a chilled bowl.

Flour squid and sliced celery at once, and blend with a fork.

Add squid and sliced celery to batter and blend thoroughly, working from the bottom of the bowl upward.

Using a large spoon, working gently from the edges of the pan, lower fritter into the oil.

With a fork, lightly spread the center of the mass to promote even doneness and crispness.

4. Flour squid and combine with sliced celery. Add squid mixture to batter.
5. With a large spoon, fry about 1/4 of the squid mixture until crisp and done. Break up the center of the mass slightly with a fork to promote thorough cooking. Repeat with the remaining batter. Drain. If the amount of frying oil is small, fry two fritters at a time for from 3 to 4 minutes. Turn once.
6. Serve together with squid tempura.
    Fritters should be broad, flat, and light, not hard round balls.

Jako and Onion Fritters *(8 fritters)*

Though small, *jako*, sardine fry that have been boiled and dried, are rich in protein, phosphorus, calcium, and iron. They make a very tasty tempura fritter that, while of course best immediately after frying, may be reheated in an oven.

>   1 oz (½ cup) *jako*
>   2 onions (medium)
>   Oil for frying
>   Salt
>   Lemon wedges
>   *Batter:*
>   1 egg and chilled water to make 1 cup
>   1 cup flour

1. Peel onions. Cut in half vertically, remove core, and slice crosswise.
2. In a chilled bowl, lightly beat egg. Blend in chilled water. Add flour all at once. Mix quickly with a fork. Ignore small lumps.
3. Add chopped onion and *jako* to batter.
4. Heat oil to 325°–350° F. Using a large spoon, drop batter for 3 or 4 fritters into oil. Each fritter should employ 1/8 of total batter. Spread the center of each with a fork to promote even cooking. Fry for from 3 to 4 minutes, turning once. Remove from oil and drain on a wire rack or paper towels.
5. Spread paper napkins in a serving dish. Arrange fritters on them, sprinkle with salt, and garnish with lemon wedges.

Shrimp and Watercress Fritters *(8 fritters)*

Fried together in this fashion, watercress—or celery leaves—and shrimp richly complement each other.

>   ½ lb shrimp
>   1 small onion (2 cups sliced)
>   Watercress (or celery leaves)
>   2 Tbsp flour
>   Oil for frying
>   Salt
>   Lemon wedges

Batter:
   1 egg and chilled water to make 1 cup
   1 cup flour

1.   Shell and devein shrimp. Peel and halve onion vertically. Remove core and slice crosswise. Chop watercress or celery leaves. Coat these ingredients with 2 Tbsp flour.
2.   In a chilled bowl, lightly beat egg and add chilled water. Add flour all at once and blend briefly with a fork, ignoring small lumps.
3.   Add shrimp and vegetables to batter.
4.   Heat oil to 325°–350° F. Using a large spoon, drop batter for 3 or 4 fritters into oil. Each fritter should employ 1/8 of total batter. Spread the center of each with a fork to promote even cooking. Fry for from 3 to 4 minutes, turning once. Remove from oil and drain on a wire rack or paper towels.
5.   Spread paper napkins in a serving dish. Arrange fritters on them, sprinkle with salt, and garnish with lemon wedges.

Crab and *Wakame* Fritters *(8 fritters)*

   4 oz crab meat (or crab-flavored *kamaboko*)
   1½ Tbsp dried, cut *wakame* (softened, ½ cup)
   Celery leaves
   2 Tbsp flour
   Oil for frying
   Salt
   Lemon wedges
Batter:
   Egg and chilled water to make ¼ cup
   ¼ cup flour

1.   Break crab meat apart with fork. Soften *wakame* in water for 5 minutes. Drain. Squeeze out as much moisture as possible. Chop celery leaves. Coat these ingredients with 2 Tbsp flour.
2.   In a chilled bowl, lightly beat egg and add chilled water. Add flour all at once and blend briefly with a fork, ignoring small lumps.
3.   Add crab, *wakame*, and celery leaves to batter.
4.   Heat oil to 325°–350° F. Using a large spoon, drop batter for 3 or 4 fritters into oil. Each fritter should employ 1/8 of total batter. Spread the center of each with a fork to promote even cooking. Fry for from 3 to 4 minutes, turning once. Remove from oil and drain on a wire rack or paper towels.
5.   Spread paper napkins in a serving dish. Arrange fritters on them, sprinkle with salt, and garnish with lemon wedges.

Roasting and Baking

Salt-baked Horse Mackerel
with Watercress (p. 87)

The old-fashioned Japanese way of roasting fish is on skewers or wire racks direct-ly over open fire. But modern housewives dislike the smoke and smell associated with this method and prefer broiling in ovens. Nevertheless, the traditional philosophy of broiling with a strong, distant heat that does not burn the fish remains sound. Broiling for a short time with a strong heat not too close to the surface browns fish in an appetizing way. Slow broiling with a weak heat, on the other hand, dries the fish and produces an unappealing white appearance.

Another piece of folk wisdom has it that roasting fish should be entrusted to a feudal lord, while roasting *mochi* glutinous rice cakes should be done by a beggar. The calm, self-important feudal lord will condescend to turn the fish only once during the roasting process, thus preserving both its natural juices and its shape. The hungry beggar may turn the *mochi* as often as he likes since it has no juices and is tough enough to keep its shape. When roasting over charcoal out of doors, too, turn fish only once. To prevent sticking, oil broiler racks and grills.

For the sake of appetizing appearance, when roasting on a wire rack or skewers, brown what will be the upper surface first then turn and cook till done. Tradi-tionally, this is the side that is up when the head is on your left and the belly side forward. Reverse the procedure when broiling below a heat source.

The following are the major Japanese ways of roasting fish and other seafoods.

Shioyaki (Salt roast)
This method brings out the natural flavors of the fish, which generally should be very fresh. If the fish is not of the freshest, increase the amount of salt slightly. Use 1/2 tsp for every 1 3/4 lb of whole fish and 2/3 tsp for every pound of fillets. Since salting causes fish to exude fluids, drain them in a colander. Roast or broil as explained above.

Teriyaki (Glossy roast)
Before roasting, the fish is marinated for 20 or 30 minutes in a sauce. During

roasting, this same sauce is brushed on the fish several times, resulting in a glossy surface—hence the name. The heat should be weaker than the one used for salt roasting because the sauce coating the fish tends to scorch easily.

Kogane-yaki (Golden roast)

The name derives from the gold color of the egg-glaze applied to fillets, shrimp, or squid before roasting. This glaze is made from 1 egg yolk plus 1 tsp sakè (or sherry), and 1/4 tsp salt. It is brushed on the fish, which is roasted till the glaze dries. The process is repeated 2 or 3 times.

Yūan-yaki (Yūan roast)

The name derives from that of a famous tea master Kitamura Yūan. Fish is marinated for 20 or 30 minutes in a marinade of soy sauce, sakè, and *mirin* before roasting. Fish prepared in this way is often served as part of the tea-ceremony meal, or *kaiseki*.

Over a charcoal barbecue fire, fillets 2/3 in thick cook in from 6 to 8 minutes and steaks 1 in thick in less than 10 minutes. Never overcook crustaceans like shrimp, lobster, or crab. Remove from the heat source as soon as the translucent flesh turns white. Oysters and clams may be cooked on the half shell. Or you may snip the hinges of clam shells and cook until steam rises from them.

Baked Cod with Soy Sauce and Lemon *(Serves 4)*

Oven-baked cod with ginger and garlic served with lemon and soy sauce is especially delicious with hot steamed rice. You may substitute bass, sea bream, mackerel, rainbow trout, or salmon for cod.

> **1 lb cod fillet**
> **Salt**
> **2 Tbsp sakè or sherry**
> **2 Tbsp salad oil**
> **½ Tbsp chopped ginger root**
> **½ Tbsp crushed garlic**
> **4 scallions (white part), sliced**
> **1 Tbsp lemon juice**
> **1½ Tbsp soy sauce**

1. Check fillet for bones. Cut into 4 equal parts. Sprinkle with salt and sakè or sherry and allow to stand for 30 minutes.
2. Heat oven to 400° F. Line a baking pan with oven paper or aluminum foil coated with salad oil. Wipe cod with paper towels. Place in lined pan and bake for 10 minutes uncovered.
3. Heat salad oil in a frying pan. In it sauté ginger, garlic, and scallions, taking care not to scorch. Remove from heat. Add lemon juice and soy sauce.
4. Arrange baked fish on a serving dish and top with sauce and vegetables.

Cod Parmigiano *(Serves 4)*

You may substitute bass, halibut, flounder, or sea bream for the cod.

> **1 lb cod**
> **Salt**
> **⅓ cup milk**
> **Butter**
> **⅓ cup bread crumbs**
> **2 Tbsp Parmesan cheese**
> **Garlic powder**
> **Chopped parsley**
> **Chopped basil**

1. Preheat oven to 375°F. Cut cod into 4 slices. Salt and allow to stand in milk for 30 minutes. Drain well.
2. Butter an ovenproof casserole.
3. Combine bread crumbs, Parmesan cheese, and garlic powder. Dredge cod slices in this mixture.
4. Arrange cod slices in casserole. Dot with 2 Tbsp butter. Bake in preheated oven for 15 to 20 minutes. Finish with a topping of chopped fresh parsley and basil.

Swordfish *Teriyaki* *(Serves 4)*

This *teriyaki* uses the Yūan sauce mentioned on p. 82. If marinating time is long, increase the amount of sakè 1.5 times. You may substitute yellowtail, sea bream, bass, mackerel, Spanish mackerel, or salmon for swordfish.

> **1 lb swordfish fillet**
> **Broccoli for garnish**
> *Yūan Marinade:*
>   **3 Tbsp soy sauce**
>   **3 Tbsp sakè**
>   **1 Tbsp *mirin* (optional)**

1. Cut swordfish into 4 equal steaks.
2. Combine Yūan marinade ingredients. Marinate fish in this mixture for an hour.
3. Place swordfish on an oiled broiler rack over a pan of water, which must not come into contact with the fish. Broil for about 3 minutes on 1 side. Turn and broil for another 4 minutes. During broiling, brush marinade on fish once or twice.
4. Arrange fish on serving platter and garnish with steamed or boiled broccoli.

Broiled Salmon with Sesame and Ginger *(Serves 4)*

Ginger makes this an interesting and delicious addition to outdoor barbecues. You may substitute yellowtail, bonito, mackerel, horse mackerel, swordfish, tuna, or shark for salmon.

> **4 (6 oz) salmon steaks**
> **2 Tbsp sesame oil**
> **¼ cup sakè or sherry**
> **2 Tbsp lemon juice**
> **2 Tbsp ginger juice**
> **Salad oil**
> **1 Tbsp soy sauce**
> **2 Tbsp sesame oil**
> **Radishes**

1.   With a wire whip or rotary egg beater, in a bowl, blend sesame oil, sakè, lemon juice, and ginger. Marinate salmon in this for 1 hour in the refrigerator. Turn from time to time.
2.   Place fish on an oiled broiler rack over water, which must not come into contact with fish. Broil on 1 side from 3 to 4 minutes. Turn, brush with marinade, and broil another 3 to 4 minutes.
3.   Arrange broiled fish on a serving platter and top with soy sauce and sesame oil blended together with a wire whip or rotary egg beater. Garnish with radishes.

Baked Salmon with Garlic *(Serves 4)*

This too is a welcome treat at outdoor barbecues. You may substitute bonito, mackerel, scallops, tuna, yellowtail, or swordfish for salmon.

> **4 (6 oz) salmon steaks**
> **2 Tbsp sakè or sherry**
> **3 Tbsp soy sauce**
> **½ tsp ginger juice**
> **1 tsp crushed garlic**
> **Salad oil**
> **Zucchini sauté**

1.   Combine sakè, soy sauce, ginger juice, and garlic in a bowl. Marinate salmon steaks in this mixture for 2 hours outside or 4 hours inside refrigerator.
2.   Place salmon on oiled broiler rack over a pan of water, which must not come into contact with fish. Broil for from 3 to 4 minutes on 1 side. Turn, brush marinade on fish and broil for another 3 to 4 minutes.
3.   Arrange on a serving platter and garnish with zucchini prepared as follows.

Zucchini Sauté

> **2 zucchini (small)**
> **1 Tbsp salad oil**
> **1 clove garlic, crushed**
> **¼ tsp salt**
> **¼ tsp dried oregano**

1. Slice zucchini in 1/8-in rounds.
2. Heat salad oil in a frying pan. Add zucchini, crushed garlic, salt, and oregano. Cover and cook for from 10 to 12 minutes over a low heat, stirring from time to time. Overcooking makes zucchini mushy.

Broiled Swordfish with Dill *(Serves 4)*

The combination of dill and soy sauce is unusual and delicious. If you are busy, the fish may be marinated the day ahead. You may substitute bonito, salmon, yellowtail, sea bream, shark, Spanish mackerel, or scallops for swordfish.

> **1 lb swordfish fillet**
> **2 Tbsp salad oil**
> **¼ cup sakè or sherry**
> **2 Tbsp lemon juice**
> **4 scallions (white part)**
> **1 Tbsp soy sauce**
> **2 Tbsp sesame oil**
> **Chopped fresh dill**
> **Lemon or lime wedges**

1. Cut the swordfish into 4 equal steaks. In a bowl, with a wire whip or rotary egg beater, blend salad oil, sakè, and lemon juice. Marinate fish in this mixture for 30 minutes, turning occasionally.
2. Cut scallions in jullienne strips and soak in cold water. Drain.
3. Place salmon on an oiled broiler rack over a pan of water, which must not come into contact with the fish. Broil from 3 to 4 minutes on 1 side. Turn and broil another 3 to 4 minutes.
4. Arrange fish on a serving platter. Combine soy sauce and sesame oil. Pour it over fish. Sprinkle with chopped fresh dill and scallions. Garnish with lemon or lime wedges. If you must use dried dill, rub it between your fingers to increase its fragrance. You may replace dill with sage or thyme. If powdered spices are used, add them to the marinade.

Oil-baked Halibut *(Serves 4)*

This simple dish is delicious and convenient when you are very busy. You may substitute bass, sea bream, cod, orange roughy, swordfish, or salmon for halibut.

1 lb halibut fillet
¼ tsp salt
Salad oil
4 oz *daikon* radish
Salt
Lemon wedges
8 red radishes

1.   Slice halibut into 4 equal parts. Sprinkle with 1/4 tsp salt and allow to stand for 20 minutes.
2.   Heat oven to 400° F. Line a baking pan with oven paper or oiled aluminum foil. Dry fish with paper towels. Place in pan and bake for 10 minutes, brushing with additional salad oil 2 or 3 times.
3.   Grate *daikon* radish and drain till reduced in volume by half.
4.   Arrange halibut on serving plate. Serve with salt, lemon wedges, grated *daikon* radish, and red radishes. The *daikon* radish may be flavored with a half-and-half mixture of lemon juice and soy sauce.

Bass *en Papillote* (Serves 4)

Fresh fish baked in waxed paper is a teasing and tempting treat for the table. You may substitute any other fish for bass.

¾ lb bass
Salt
Pepper
½ cup milk
1 Tbsp white wine
8 stalks green asparagus
1 oz butter
Chopped parsley
Lemon wedges
Waxed paper

1.   Preheat oven to 350°F. Cut cod into 4 slices. Sprinkle with salt and pepper. Allow to stand in milk for 20 minutes. Wipe dry. Sprinkle with white wine.
2.   Cut off and discard hard segments of asparagus stalks. Cut into half.
3.   Cut waxed paper into heart shapes that will accommodate cod slices. Butter 1 side of paper, leaving an unbuttered rim all round. Place a slice of cod on one half of each piece of paper. Top each slice of fish with asparagus and a sprinkling of chopped parsley. Forcing out as much air as possible, fold other half of paper over fish. Double fold edges to secure in place.
3.   Bake in preheated oven 10 minutes.
4.   Serve garnished with lemon wedges.

Oven-baked Mackerel with Scallions and Ginger *(Serves 4 to 6)*

Mackerel is rich in the nonsaturated oil called EPA, which helps prevent cardiac infarction. The Shimane Medical School has reported that eating it regularly for 2 weeks noticeably lowers blood-cholesterol counts. Herring, sardines, and salmon too have high EPA content. Their effectiveness in cholesterol control, however, depends on freshness.

You may substitute bass, salmon, or rainbow trout for mackerel.

2 mackerel (1¼ lb each)
⅔ tsp salt
Pepper
10 scallions
2 ginger-root slices
2 Tbsp sesame oil
2 Tbsp soy sauce

1. Preheat oven to 400°F. Clean and wash mackerel (see p. 130). Sprinkle with salt and pepper and allow to stand in a colander for 20 minutes.
2. Julienne cut white parts of scallions and ginger-root slices.
3. Line a baking pan with oven paper or oiled aluminum foil. Place fish in pan and bake for 20 minutes.
4. Remove from oven. Discard oil and juices from pan. Tilt pan and allow it to stand for 10 minutes. Discard juices that accumulate.
5. Prepare dressing by beating sesame oil in a bowl as you gradually add soy sauce.
6. Arrange fish on a serving platter. Top with scallions and ginger and serve with dressing.

Salt-baked Horse Mackerel with Watercress *(Serves 4)*

This time-saving cooking method emphasizes the natural flavors of the fish. Whole fish are better than steaks or fillets for salt-baking. You may substitute bass, halibut, herring, mackerel, Spanish mackerel, sea bream, salmon, sole, or trout for horse mackerel.

4 horse mackerel (1¾ lb in all)
½ tsp salt
Sweet green peppers
Salad oil
Watercress
Lemon wedges

1. Clean and wash horse mackerel (see p. 130). Dry well with paper towels, and

sprinkle lightly, inside and out, with salt. Protect fins and tail from burning by wrapping them in aluminum foil.

2.   Wash and quarter green peppers.

3.   Place horse mackerel on an oiled broiler rack over a pan of water, which must not come in contact with fish.

4.   Before broiling determine which side will be up at serving time. Begin by broiling the underside—about 4 in from the heating unit. Turn and broil the upper side. Immediately before the fish is done, remove aluminum foil and brown fins and tail. Broil green peppers for 2 minutes together with fish. Brush them with salad oil and turn them once during broiling.

5.   Arrange horse mackerel in the center of a serving dish. Place broiled green peppers and watercress in front of it and serve with lemon wedges.

Rainbow Trout Baked in Herbs *(Serves 4)*

A light and fragrant delight.

> **4 rainbow trout**
> **Salt**
> **⅓ cup white wine**
> **Fresh ginger root**
> **Chopped parsley**
> **Chopped celery leaves**
> **Salad oil**
> **Lemon wedges**

1.   Preheat oven to 350°F. Clean trout, discarding head and tail. Wash and dry well. Sprinkle with salt and white wine and allow to stand for 20 minutes.

2.   Dry trout thoroughly. Slice some of ginger and julienne cut the rest. Reserving some parsley, celery leaves, and julienne-cut ginger, stuff body cavities with parsley, celery leaves, and sliced ginger.

3.   Wrap trout in oiled aluminum foil. Bake in preheated oven for 15 to 20 minutes. Open foil and lightly brown fish.

4.   Serve sprinkled with more chopped parsley, chopped celery leaves, and julienne-cut ginger. Garnish with lemon wedges.

Gold-roast Red Sea Bream *(Serves 4)*

The golden glaze on the red sea bream is opulent to the eye and delicate to the taste. You may substitute turbot, halibut, bass, orange roughy, squid, or shrimp for sea bream.

> **1 lb sea-bream fillet**
> **Salt**
> **2 Tbsp sakè**

Green asparagus
Salad oil
2 egg yolks
$\frac{1}{2}$ Tbsp sakè

1.   Preheat oven to 375°F. Cut fillet into 4 equal parts. Sprinkle with salt and sakè and allow to stand for 10 minutes.
2.   Snap off tough lower sections of asparagus stalks. Steam or boil till crisp-tender.
3.   Line a baking pan with oven paper or oiled aluminum foil. Dry fish with paper towels, place in pan, and bake for from 7 to 8 minutes. Do not allow it to color.
4.   With paper towels wipe away oil that appears on surface of fish. Combine egg yolks and sakè and brush mixture on surface of fish. Return to oven. When egg glaze has dried, remove from oven and repeat the process.
5.   Arrange fish on a serving platter and garnish with green asparagus.

Gold-roast Squid *(Serves 4)*

Alternating gold and white are an attractive color scheme. Overcooking toughens squid, which is done when it has turned opaque.

2 squid
Milk
1 egg yolk
1 tsp sakè or sherry
Salt
Watercress

1.   Clean squid (see p. 133). Remove tentacles. Make an incision in one side, open body and remove inner membrane.
2.   Score the outer surface with shallow incisions 1/4 in apart. Turn and score again to make a checkerboard pattern. Cut into 1 1/2 in squares. Allow to stand in milk for 20 minutes.
3.   Combine egg yolk and sakè.
4.   Remove squid from milk, dry, and salt lightly. Broil, 8 in from heat source, scored side up. Turn and lightly broil underside. Remove half the squid squares to a serving plate and keep warm.
5.   Brush egg glaze on the upper (scored) surfaces of remaining squares and return them to the oven to dry. Repeat process.
6.   Arrange white and gold squid squares attractively on a serving plate and serve garnished with watercress.

Squid *Teriyaki* (*Serves 4*)

This is delicious prepared either in an oven or on a barbecue grill. Take care not to overcook.

> **2 squid**
> **Celery sticks**
> *Sauce:*
> ⅓ **cup soy sauce**
> ⅓ **cup *mirin* (sweetened sakè)**

1.   Preheat oven to 400°F. Clean squid (see p. 133). Discard innards. Cut off tentacles and trim off suction cups.
2.   Stuff body cavity with trimmed legs and close opening with toothpicks. Make shallow, crosswise incisions in the body at an interval of about 2/3 in.
3.   Combine sauce ingredients in a saucepan. Bring to a boil and remove from heat. Briefly roast in heated oven. Remove from oven and brush with sauce. Return to oven to dry. Repeat this process 2 or 3 times.
4.   Cut into rings along previously made incisions. Serve garnished with celery sticks.

Supper Dishes

Shrimp in Tomato
Sauce (p. 99)

Cod Paprika *(Serves 4)*

The combination of the deep red of paprika and the white of sour cream looks as
delicious as it is. You may substitute sardines, pike, bass, bonito, halibut, turbot,
herring, mackerel, horse mackerel, sea bream, swordfish, tuna, or yellowtail for
cod.

>**1 lb cod**
>**¼ tsp salt**
>**2 Tbsp vegetable oil**
>**½ cup chopped onion**
>**1 clove crushed garlic**
>**Pepper**
>**½ cup tomato sauce**
>**1 tsp paprika**
>**½ cup chicken broth**
>**2 Tbsp milk**
>**2 Tbsp sour cream**
>**Fried potatoes for garnish**

1. Skin and bone cod. Cut into 8 equal slices. Sprinkle with salt and allow to
drain in a colander for 20 minutes.
2. Heat 1 Tbsp vegetable oil in a frying pan. In it lightly sauté onions and garlic.
Transfer to a pan.
3. Dry cod and sprinkle with pepper. Heat another 1 Tbsp vegetable oil in the pan
in which onions were sautéed and brown cod on both sides in it. The fish need not
be done at this stage. Remove fish in the pan in which onions and garlic were
transferred.
4. In the same frying pan, using a wooden spoon, combine tomato sauce, paprika, and chicken broth. Bring to a boil and remove from heat. Pour over cod
in pan. Cover pan with a lid and simmer over a low heat for 10 minutes. With
a spatula, lift fish from time to time to prevent sticking. Correct seasoning.

5. Using a rotary egg beater, gradually add milk to sour cream. Blend thoroughly.

6. Arrange fish on a serving plate. Top with paprika sauce. Pour sour-cream mixture over it. Serve garnished with fried potatoes. Frozen ones are convenient.

Baked Cod in Radish Sauce *(Serves 4)*

The appearance of grated *daikon* radish gives to this and other similar dishes the name *mizorè*, which means sleet. In this refreshing combination, the grated radish greatly enhances the flavor of cod. You may substitute sardines, bonito, halibut, herring, mackerel, horse mackerel, sea bream, or yellowtail for cod.

> **1 lb cod fillet**
> **³/₄ tsp salt**
> **4 Tbsp sakè**
> **²/₃ lb *daikon* radish**
> **¹/₂ cup stock (pp. 37–39) or chicken broth**
> ***Daikon*-radish sprouts or alfalfa sprouts**

1. Preheat oven to 350°F. Skin and bone fish and cut into 8 equal slices. Sprinkle with 1/4 tsp salt and 2 Tbsp sakè and allow to stand for 30 minutes.

2. Peel *daikon*, grate it, and allow it to drain in a colander till reduced in volume by half. Heating radish removes its peppery taste.

3. Mix stock, 2 Tbsp sakè, and 1/2 tsp salt and bring to a boil.

4. Arrange cod in an oven-proof dish and top with grated *daikon* radish. Pour on hot stock mixture. Cover with aluminum foil. Bake for 10 minutes.

6. Sprinkle with *daikon*-radish sprouts or alfalfa sprouts and serve at once. The recipe may be prepared as far as step *3* well in advance of baking time. Using a combination of different fishes makes this good dish even better.

Halibut and Tofu Casserole *(Serves 4)*

This simple baked dish requires only one casserole. You may substitute bonito, mackerel, horse mackerel, or salmon for halibut.

> **1 lb halibut**
> **¹/₃ tsp salt**
> **¹/₄ cup milk**
> **1 block tofu**
> **¹/₂ tsp salt**
> **4 scallions (white part)**
> **1 Tbsp sakè or sherry**
> **1 Tbsp salad oil**
> **1 Tbsp white sesame seeds**

1. Preheat oven to 350°F. Skin and bone fish and cut into 8 equal slices. Sprinkle it with 1/3 tsp salt and soak in milk for 30 minutes.

2.   Drain tofu. Crumble it coarse with a rotary egg beater. Season with 1/2 tsp salt and drain in a colander for 30 minutes.

3.   Cut scallions in thin diagonal slices.

4.   Remove halibut from milk; discard milk. Arrange halibut in casserole, sprinkle with sakè and scallions, and spread drained tofu on top. Sprinkle salad oil evenly over tofu and add sesame seeds.

5.   Bake, uncovered, at 350°F for 20 minutes.

Oven-baked Seafood and Tofu *(Serves 4)*

Top your favorite seafood and chicken with a mixture of egg and tofu and bake it for a low-calorie, wholesome, and easy treat. You may use any white-flesh fish.

$\frac{1}{2}$ block tofu
4 oz halibut or other white-flesh fish
4 shrimp
4 oz skinned chicken, thigh meat
4 scallops
2 Tbsp sakè or sherry
$\frac{1}{8}$ tsp salt
$1\frac{1}{2}$ oz *enoki* mushrooms or 2 oz champignons
Celery leaves
4 eggs
$\frac{3}{4}$ tsp salt
Pepper
$1\frac{3}{4}$ tsp stock (pp. 37–39) or chicken broth

1.   Preheat oven to 310° F. Boil tofu for 30 seconds. Drain in a colander. Crumble coarse. Allow to drain again in colander for 20 minutes.

2.   Slice halibut. Shell shrimp, leaving tail-section shell intact. Devein shrimp. Slice chicken meat. Place these ingredients and scallops on a plate, sprinkle with sakè and 1/8 tsp salt, and allow to stand 20 minutes. Cut off and discard root ends of *enoki* mushrooms or slice champignons. Chop celery leaves.

3.   Using a rotary egg beater, thoroughly beat eggs. Add salt, pepper, and stock. Add tofu to this mixture and blend thoroughly with an egg beater.

4.   Wipe fish, chicken, shrimp, and scallops and place them in the bottom of a casserole (1 1/2 pt). Top with the tofu-egg mixture.

5.   Cover casserole with aluminum foil. Bake for 40 minutes. Remove cover and sprinkle with chopped celery leaves.

Lettuce-wrapped Swordfish *(Serves 4)*

Fillets of your favorite fish wrapped in lettuce leaves and steamed in the oven are delicious with steamed rice.

1 lb swordfish
1 clove garlic

2 Tbsp soy sauce
2 Tbsp sakè
3 thin slices fresh ginger root
8 leaves iceberg lettuce
Lemon wedges

1.   Preheat oven to 350°F. Cut swordfish into 8 slices. Slice garlic thin. Combine soy sauce, sakè, ginger, and garlic. Allow fish to stand in this mixture for 30 minutes.
2.   Blanch lettuce leaves for about 10 seconds. Drain.
3.   Wrap fish slices in lettuce. Arrange in casserole and top with liquor in which fish has steeped. Cover tightly with aluminum foil.
4.   Set casserole in a shallow pan containing boiling water. Bake in preheated oven for 10 minutes.
5.   Serve hot with lemon wedges.

Orange Roughy in Cauliflower-and-cheese Sauce *(Serves 4)*

⅔ lb orange roughy
Salt
Pepper
1 head cauliflower
Flour
Vinegar
2 Tbsp butter
1 Tbsp chopped parsley
Cheese Sauce:
   4 Tbsp butter
   4 Tbsp flour
   1½ cups milk
   2 Tbsp grated Parmesan cheese
   Pepper

1.   Preheat oven to 200°F. Cut orange roughy into bite-size pieces and sprinkle with salt and pepper. Steam in a little water. Drain, reserving water.
2.   Break cauliflower into small florets. Boil till crisp-tender in water to which have been added small amounts of salt, flour, and vinegar. Drain well.
3.   Melt butter in a saucepan. Add flour and stirring constantly with a wooden paddle, cook over a medium heat till thoroughly blended. Slowly add water in which fish was steamed and milk. Blend till smooth. Add grated cheese, salt, and pepper.
4.   Arrange fish and cauliflower in bottom of a buttered casserole. Pour sauce over these ingredients and dot with butter. Bake in preheated oven for from 5 to 10 minutes. Serve sprinkled with chopped parsley.

Cod and Shrimp Casserole with Potatoes *(Serves 4)*

Children love this combination of seafood, potatoes, and tomatoes with a melted-cheese topping. Prepare it ahead of time, add the cheese, and finish it off in the oven at the last minute. It is good both as a hearty luncheon dish and as a supper main course. You may substitute any white-flesh fish for cod, but do not leave the shrimp out.

$\frac{1}{2}$ lb cod fillet
$\frac{1}{2}$ lb shrimp (small)
$\frac{3}{4}$ tsp salt
$\frac{1}{2}$ cup and 2 Tbsp white wine
1 lb potatoes
$\frac{1}{2}$ (4 oz) onion
Pepper
3 Tbsp salad oil
$\frac{1}{4}$ cup coarse-chopped parsley
2 tsp crushed garlic
2 tomatoes (small)
$\frac{1}{4}$ cup bread crumbs
$\frac{1}{2}$ cup grated mozzarella cheese
2 bay leaves

1.   Preheat oven to 400°F. Skin and bone fish and slice into large bite-size pieces. Shell and devein shrimp. Sprinkle fish and shrimp with 1/4 tsp salt and 2 Tbsp white wine. Allow to stand for 20 minutes.
2.   Peel potatoes and slice into 1/4-in rounds. Spread on the bottom of a casserole. Slice onion and spread on top of potatoes. Sprinkle with 1/2 tsp salt, pepper, and 1 Tbsp salad oil.
3.   Cover casserole with aluminum foil and bake at 400°F for 30 minutes.
4.   Heat 1 Tbsp salad oil in a frying pan. In it sauté parsley and garlic.
5.   Slice tomatoes into 1/4-in rounds. Mix bread crumbs, 1 Tbsp oil, and cheese.
6.   Remove casserole from oven. Leave oven setting at 400°F.
7.   Remove aluminum foil. Arrange seafood on top of potatoes and onions. Put shrimp in the middle as they tend to dry out readily. Discard white wine in which seafood was marinated. Sprinkle parsley and garlic on top of seafood. Add bay leaves. Sprinkle 1/2 cup white wine evenly over all ingredients. Arrange tomatoes on top. Cover with bread-crumb mixture. Re-cover with aluminum foil and return to oven for 15 minutes. Remove aluminum foil and continue cooking till crumb topping is brown and seafood is done.
8.   Sprinkle cheese over top and return to oven till cheese has melted. Serve at once.

Haddock and Potato Gratin *(Serves 4)*

This filling dish is another favorite with young people. You may substitute scallops, shrimp, or any other white-flesh fish for haddock.

1 lb haddock fillet
1 lb potatoes
Salt
1 cup milk
2 Tbsp butter or margarine
$\frac{1}{3}$ tsp salt
White pepper
$\frac{1}{2}$ tsp crushed garlic
2 Tbsp salad oil
$\frac{1}{2}$ cup grated mozzarella cheese
Chopped parsley

1. Preheat oven to 350°F. Slice haddock fillet into bite-size pieces, sprinkle with salt, and allow to stand for 20 minutes.
2. Combine milk, butter or margarine, salt, white pepper, and garlic in a sauce-pan. Bring to a boil and remove from heat.
3. Peel potatoes and slice into 1/4-in rounds, adding them to the milk mixture as they are sliced, without washing them. Cover pan and simmer over a low heat for 10 minutes, taking care not to scorch. Transfer potatoes to a casserole.
4. Dry fish, sprinkle with white pepper, and soak in salad oil. Arrange fish on top of potatoes in casserole. Discard oil in which fish was soaked. Bake casserole, uncovered, at 350°F for 25 minutes or until fish is done. Sprinkle with cheese and return to oven until cheese has melted. Sprinkle with chopped parsley and serve at once.

Rainbow Trout Meunière with Paprika and Almonds *(Serves 4)*

Substitute fillets of your favorite fish in this dish, which is enhanced by the fragrance of almonds and the fresh green of parsley.

4 rainbow trout
Salt
Pepper
$\frac{1}{4}$ cup milk
Flour
3 Tbsp salad oil
1 Tbsp white wine
$\frac{1}{3}$ tsp paprika
4 Tbsp butter
1 cup slivered, blanched almonds
Parsley
Lemon wedges

1. Clean trout, discarding heads and tails (see p. 130). Wash and dry well.
2. Sprinkle with salt and pepper and allow to stand in milk for 30 minutes.
3. Dry again. Coat inside and out with flour, taking care to shake off excess.

4.   In a frying pan, heat salad oil. Over a high heat, begin frying the sides of the fish that will be exposed when served. Shake the pan gently to prevent sticking. When browned and half done, turn the fish. Lower the heat and continue cooking till completely done. Sprinkle fish with white wine. Cover pan and steam for from 1 to 2 minutes. Remove to a serving plate and sprinkle with paprika. Keep warm.
5.   In a separate pan, heat butter. Over a medium heat, brown almonds in butter. Sprinkle almonds on fish. Serve at once with parsley and lemon wedges.

Cod in Milk *(Serves 4)*

A fast and easy supper dish in which cooking in milk masks fishy odors.

> **1 lb cod**
> **⅓ cup milk**
> **⅓ cup water**
> **Salt**
> **Butter**
> **Chopped parsley**
> **Lemon wedges**
> **Boiled potatoes**
> **Carrot glacé**

1.   Cut cod into 8 slices.
2.   Combine milk and water and heat. Add salt. Arrange cod slices in a shallow pan. Pour milk mixture over them. Cover with waxed paper and simmer for 10 minutes. Remove from heat and allow to stand covered for 5 minutes.
3.   Arrange fish on a serving dish. Top with thin, square pats of butter and chopped parsley. Serve with lemon wedges, boiled potatoes, and carrot glacé.

Note: Cut waxed paper to fit the pan. Make a cross of 1-in incisions in the middle. The paper lid ensures that fish remains submerged during cooking.

Sardines in Ginger Sauce *(Serves 4)*

The full-bodied flavors of this dish go well with plain steamed rice.

> **16 fresh sardines**
> **1 oz fresh ginger root**
> **¼ cup sakè**
> **¼ cup water**
> **2 Tbsp sugar**
> **3 Tbsp soy sauce**

1.   Clean sardines, discarding heads. Cut in 1-in lengths.
2.   Julienne cut ginger, reserving a small amount for garnish.
3.   Arrange sardines in a saucepan. Sprinkle ginger over the fish. Add sakè and

water and bring to a boil. Add sugar and soy sauce. Cover with a paper lid, return to the boil, and simmer gently over a low heat.

4. When almost all liquid has evaporated, remove fish from pan, arrange on a serving plate, and top with julienne-cut ginger.

Note: Cut paper to fit the pan. Make a cross of 1-in incisions in the middle. The paper lid ensures that fish remains submerged during cooking.

Swordfish Simmered in Tomatoes *(Serves 4)*

Practically everyone loves tomato-flavored main dishes. This one is especially worth preparing since swordfish is rich in high-quality protein that relieves stress and helps prevent aging. You may, however, substitute bonito, cod, halibut, herring, mackerel, horse mackerel, shark, or sea bream for swordfish.

> **1 lb swordfish fillet**
> **1 Tbsp vegetable oil**
> **1 tsp crushed garlic**
> **2 Tbsp brandy**
> **4 (2 lb) tomatoes**
> **3 Tbsp chopped scallions**
> **¾ cup white wine**
> **1 chicken bouillon cube**
> **Juice of 1 lemon**
> **Salt**
> **Pepper**
> **Cayenne pepper or chili pepper**
> **Watercress or fresh mint leaves**

1. Skin and bone fish and cut it into 12 bite-size pieces.
2. In a frying pan, heat vegetable oil. In it sauté garlic, taking care not to scorch. Add swordfish to pan and brown on one side. Turn. Sprinkle with brandy and ignite to burn off alcohol.
3. Peel and seed tomatoes. Dice into cubes about 1/2 in to a side. Combine with scallions, white wine, bouillon cube, and lemon juice and pour over fish. Cover pan and simmer for 3 minutes.
4. Remove fish from pan and keep warm. Season sauce with salt, pepper, and cayenne pepper, stirring constantly with a wooden spoon.
5. Pour half of tomato sauce into a serving plate. Add swordfish. Pour remaining sauce on top and sprinkle with watercress or fresh mint leaves.

Cod Creole *(Serves 4)*

Be sure to use fresh tomatoes in this simple, but very appetizing dish. It is good prepared in advance and reheated at dinner time. You may substitute halibut, pike, bass, hake, turbot, orange roughy, sea bream, sole, swordfish, or shrimp for cod.

> **1 lb cod fillet**
> **½ tsp salt**
> **1 (⅗ lb) tomato (large)**
> **1 sweet green pepper**
> **2 oz onion**
> **1 Tbsp lemon juice**
> **2 Tbsp white wine**
> **1 Tbsp salad oil**
> **Basil**
> **White pepper**
> **4–5 drops Tabasco**

1. Skin and bone cod, sprinkle with 1/4 tsp salt, and allow to drain in a colander for 20 minutes.
2. Peel and seed tomato. Dice it fine. Seed green pepper. Dice it and onion fine.
3. In a saucepan, combine cod; remaining salt; and lemon juice, white wine, and salad oil. Add tomato and onion. Finally add basil, white pepper, and tabasco.
4. Bring to a boil; lower heat; and simmer, covered, for from 13 to 15 minutes. top with shrimp.

Shrimp in Tomato Sauce *(Serves 4)*

Easy to make, yet festive, this dish is good for the health because the taurin in shrimp helps lower blood-cholesterol levels.

> **2 lb shrimp (large, with heads remaining)**
> **Salt**
> **Pepper**
> **1 stalk celery**
> **1 onion (small)**
> **1 carrot**
> **2 Tbsp salad oil**
> **1 clove sliced garlic**
> **⅓ cup tomato paste**
> **1 bay leaf**
> **Thyme**
> **1 stalk parsley**
> **½ cup white wine**
> **2 cups water**
> **Salt**
> **1 tsp flour**
> **1 tsp butter or margarine**
> **Fresh or frozen spinach for garnish**

1. Devein shrimp. Wash and dry. Sprinkle with salt and pepper.
2. Slice celery, onion, and carrot thin. In a frying pan, heat salad oil and sauté these vegetables plus sliced garlic in it. Add shrimp and, turning it frequently, sauté till the shells are red on both sides. Add tomato paste, bay leaf, thyme, parsley, white wine, water, and salt and simmer for 5 minutes. Remove shrimp. Simmer sauce an additional 10 minutes.
3. Work flour and butter or margarine into a smooth paste with the tips of the fingers. Drop this, a little at a time, into the simmering sauce. Stirring constantly, continue cooking till the sauce has thickened. Strain sauce through a metal strainer, pressing vegetables with the back of a wooden spoon to extract as much as possible.
4. Briefly boil spinach. Wring out as much water as possible and cut into 2-in lengths.
5. Pour tomato sauce into a serving platter. Arrange spinach in the center, and top with shrimp.

Hints. Overcooking toughens shrimp. The heads enrich both the flavor and the color of the sauce.

Seafood and Rice

Sashimi Rice (p. 109)

● *Cooking Rice the Japanese Way*

Japanese-style rice is most delicious when it has been removed from the heat after boiling and has been allowed to steam, covered, for 10 minutes. For Japanese cooking, always use short-grain rice. The secret to success begins with the washing.

First put the measured rice in a colander set in a somewhat larger bowl. Fill the bowl with water and wash the rice vigorously and quickly with your hand. Lift the colander out and discard the milky water in the bowl. Repeat 2 or 3 times until the water remaining in the bowl is clear. Leave the rice in the colander to drain for 20 minutes. The rice may be washed in the bowl without the colander and the wash water may be gently poured off. Repeat this several times and drain for 20 minutes.

● *Amount of Water for Steaming*

Use 10 percent more water than the volume of the rice. For instance, for 4 cups rice use 4 2/5 cups water.

● *Pot*

Modern automatic rice cookers have eliminated the worry and fear of failure from the process. If you do not have one, select a heavy pot with a close-fitting lid.

● *Heat Control*

If you are using an automatic cooker, follow the maker's instructions. If you are using a heavy pot, first bring the correct amount of water to a boil. Add the measured, washed, and drained rice all at once. Or you may combine rice and water from the outset and bring them to the boil together. Although proportions remain the same, the former method is generally used for large amounts.

■ *For 4 cups*

Measure 4 cups of short-grain rice. Wash according to procedures described on preceding page and allow to drain for 20 minutes. Combine in heavy, deep pot with 4 2/5 cups water. Cover and bring to a boil: from 5 to 6 minutes over a medium heat. Turn heat to low and continue cooking from 8 to 9 more minutes. Remove from heat. Allow to stand, covered, for 10 minutes.

■ *For 8 cups*

Measure 8 cups short-grain rice. Wash according to procedures described on preceding page and allow to drain for 20 minutes. In a large, heavy pan bring to the boil 8 4/5 cups water. Add rice and stir well with a wooden spoon. Cover and boil for 1 minute. Turn heat to low and cook for from 13 to 15 minutes. Remove from heat and allow to stand, covered, for 15 minutes.

■ *For 1 cup*

Wash and drain 1 cup short-grain rice. Allow to stand for 20 minutes. In a heavy saucepan with a close-fitting lid, combine rice and 1 1/10 cups water. Over a medium heat, bring to the boil. Turn heat to low and continue cooking for from 12 to 14 minutes. Remove from heat and allow to stand, covered, for from 7 to 8 minutes.

• *After Cooking*

When steamed rice has stood for the prescribed period, lightly break it up with a wooden spoon or, preferably, the wooden serving paddle known as a *shamoji*. Cover with cheesecloth while it is warm. After it is cold, the lid of the cooking pot or kitchen wrap is sufficient. Leftover steamed rice may be stored in the refrigerator, wrapped in kitchen wrap, for from 2 to 3 days. Or it may be stored in plastic bags in the freezer. In the latter case, flatten the mass of rice somewhat. Frozen leftover rice may be very successfully rewarmed in a microwave oven.

• *Oven-steamed Rice*

With an oven-proof glass container it is possible to prepare perfect steamed rice in the oven without being worried about doneness.

3 cups rice
$3\frac{1}{3}$ cups hot water

1. Preheat oven to 475°F. Place rice in a colander set in a slightly larger bowl. Under the tap, wash rice in running water as explained on preceding page. Repeat 2 or 3 times.
2. Allow rice to drain in the colander for 20 minutes.

3. Put drained rice in an oven-proof glass bowl. Add 3 1/3 cups hot water. Cover with aluminum foil.

4. Cook in preheated oven for 15 minutes or until water has almost entirely evaporated. Turn oven off.

5. Leave bowl, covered, in oven for 10 minutes.

6. With a large spoon or the traditional *shamoji* rice paddle, lightly break rice up. Cover with aluminum foil to keep moist.

Confetti Sushi *(30 balls)*

Colorful sushi balls for parties. The recipe explains the preparation of sushi rice, on which many variations may be worked.

3 cups rice
1 4-in square *kombu*
3 cups water
$\frac{1}{2}$ lb deveined shrimp
6 Tbsp rice vinegar
$2\frac{1}{8}$ tsp salt
$\frac{1}{8}$ tsp soy sauce
4 oz frozen mixed vegetables (peas, carrots, corn)
$\frac{2}{3}$ Tbsp sugar

1. Wipe both sides of *kombu* with paper towels. Combine *kombu* and water in a saucepan. Allow to stand for 10 minutes. Over a medium heat, bring to a boil. Just before the boiling point is reached, remove *kombu*.

2. Boil deveined shrimp in salted water for from 2 to 3 minutes. Drain and shell. Chop and season with mixture of 2 Tbsp vinegar, 1/8 tsp salt, and soy sauce. Allow to stand for 30 minutes.

3. Briefly boil frozen vegetables and drain in a colander.

4. Wash rice till water runs clear. Drain in a colander for 20 minutes. In a heavy pot, combine *kombu* stock made in preceding step and rice. Cover tightly. Bring to the boil and boil for 1 minute. Turn heat to low and cook an additional 10 minutes, or until almost all water has evaporated. Remove from heat and allow to stand, covered, for 10 minutes.

5. Combine 4 Tbsp rice vinegar, sugar, and 2 tsp salt.

6. Turn steamed rice out into a large bowl. With a wooden spoon or spatula, rapidly stir the rice with a downward cutting motion as you pour on the mixture of vinegar, sugar, and salt. To accelerate cooling, fan the rice with one hand as you stir, or train an electric fan on it. When it is cool and glossy, you will have rice prepared for use in many different kinds of sushi.

7. Drain shrimp and mix them and frozen vegetables with sushi rice.

8. Divide rice mixture into 30 equal balls. This is less messy to do if the sushi mixture is heaped in the center of a 6-in square of kitchen wrap which is wrapped

around it as the balls are formed. Wrap each ball in a 6-in square of kitchen wrap and tie with colorful ribbon.

Spring *Chirashi* Sushi *(Serves 4)*

Although this is traditionally served, with a clear clam broth, during the Girl's Day Festival, March 3, it is a pleasing addition to Easter parties as well, especially since it uses several eggs, long associated with the spring and the Easter festivities. You may substitute shrimp for scallops.

> **3 cups rice**
> **1 4-inch square *kombu***
> **3¼ cups water**
> **4 Tbsp rice vinegar**
> **1 Tbsp sugar**
> **2 tsp salt**
> **2 Tbsp sesame seeds**
> **4 eggs**
> **1 Tbsp water**
> **1 Tbsp cornstarch**
> **¼ tsp salt**
> **Salad oil**
> **⅓ cup frozen corn**
> **8 scallops**
> **1 Tbsp lemon juice**
> ***Daikon*-radish sprouts or alfalfa sprouts**
> **Lemon slices**

1.   Wipe both sides of *kombu* with paper towels. Combine *kombu* and 3 1/4 cups water in a saucepan. Allow to stand for 10 minutes. Over a medium heat, bring to a boil. Just before the boiling point is reached, remove *kombu* (you may substitute commercially available stock bases).
2.   Wash rice till water runs clear. Drain in a colander for 20 minutes. In a heavy pot, combine *kombu* stock made in preceding step and rice. Cover tightly. Bring to the boil and boil for 1 minute. Turn heat to low and cook an additional 8 to 9 minutes, or until almost all water has evaporated. Remove from heat and allow to stand, covered, for 10 minutes. Or you may cook the rice in the oven as explained on pp. 102–103.
3.   Combine rice vinegar, sugar, and salt.
4.   Turn steamed rice out into a large bowl. With a wooden spoon or spatula, rapidly stir the rice with a downward cutting motion as you pour on the mixture of vinegar, sugar, and salt. To accelerate cooling, fan the rice with one hand as you stir, or train an electric fan on it.
5.   In an unoiled frying pan, covered, toast sesame seeds over a low heat. Shake the pan constantly. When you hear 4 or 5 of the seeds pop—like popcorn—

remove the pan from the heat. Cracking the lid a little to let steam escape, continue shaking till the seeds have cooled.

6.   Lightly beat eggs. Blend water, cornstarch, and salt and add to eggs, stirring well. Fold a paper towel and soak it in salad oil. Heat a frying pan. Oil it with the paper towel. Pour in enough of the egg mixture to form a thin crepelike layer. Return excess egg to bowl. Dry the crepe and turn it out on a chopping board. Repeat until all egg mixture has been used. From these thin egg sheets, you may cut out whatever fancy figures you like. Chop the parts left over fine. Or you may cut all the egg sheets into thin julienne strips.

7.   Boil frozen corn and drain well.

8.   Wash scallops. If large, slice in half horizontally. Heat salad oil in a frying pan. Sauté scallops till color changes. Sprinkle with lemon juice.

9.   Cut off and discard bottoms of *daikon*-radish sprouts or alfalfa sprouts. Wash and drain. Cut in half if long.

10.   Combine sushi rice, sesame seeds, chopped egg sheets, and corn. Mound on a serving dish. If you have made fancy egg cutouts decorate the rice with them. Or sprinkle the top with julienne egg strips. Sprinkle with *daikon*-radish sprouts or alfalfa sprouts. Arrange scallops attractively around the rice and garnish with lemon slices.

Salmon Rice *(Serves 4 to 6)*

Rice mixed with flaked red salmon and scallions is flavored with sesame seeds in a dish that adds color to any party.

     3 cups rice
     ⅓ lb salmon fillet
     3 cups water
     2 Tbsp sakè
     1 tsp salt
     3 scallions, chopped
     ½ Tbsp salad oil
     ½ Tbsp sesame oil
     Lemon peel
     1 Tbsp sesame seeds
     Powdered seaweed, *aonori* (optional)

1.   Wash rice till water runs clear. Drain for 20 minutes in a colander. In a heavy pot, combine water, sakè, 1/2 tsp salt, and rice. Cover tightly and, over a medium heat, bring to a boil. Boil for 1 minute. Turn heat to low and cook for another 8 to 9 minutes or until moisture has almost entirely evaporated. Remove from heat and allow to stand, covered, for 10 minutes.

2.   Skin and bone salmon. Sprinkle with 1/2 tsp salt and allow to stand 10 minutes. Broil on both sides till done. Flake flesh fine with a fork. Mix well with chopped scallions, salad oil, and sesame oil.

3.   Chop zest only of lemon peel fine. Toast sesame seeds as preceding recipe.
4.   Combine rice and salmon mixture. Put in a deep serving bowl and top with lemon peel and toasted sesame seeds. A fine powdery seaweed product known as *aonori* is a flavorful addition to this dish. Remember that cold rice can be heated in a lidded container in a slow oven or in a microwave oven.

Shrimp Rice *(Serves 4)*

This is an easy dish, very popular with children. The only aspect of its preparation requiring attention is cooking the rice itself. This amount will serve from 6 to 8 when used as an accompaniment to hearty vegetable dishes.

> **3 cups rice**
> **3 cups water**
> **3 Tbsp sakè**
> **$\frac{1}{4}$ tsp salt**
> **$2\frac{4}{5}$ oz *sakura* dried shrimp**
> **3-in square *kombu***
> **$\frac{1}{2}$ cup frozen green peas**

1.   Wash rice till water runs clear. Drain for 20 minutes in a colander. In a heavy pot, combine water, sakè, salt, *sakura* shrimp, *kombu*, and rice. Cover tightly and, over a medium heat, bring to a boil. Boil for 1 minute. Turn heat to low and cook for another 8 to 9 minutes or until moisture has almost entirely evaporated. Remove from heat and allow to stand, covered, for 10 minutes.
2.   Quickly boil frozen green peas. Drain them. Sprinkle them on top of the cooked rice and mix gently. Hard cheese (Monterey Jack, for instance) may be cut to dice the size of the peas and mixed with the rice.

Rice with Horse Mackerel *(Serves 4)*

Sesame seeds and lemon give added zest to this mixture of steamed rice and flaked, salt-roasted horse mackerel. You may substitute sea bream, pike, or grunt for horse mackerel.

> **3 cups rice**
> **1 lb horse mackerel**
> **$\frac{1}{3}$ tsp salt**
> **3 cups water**
> **2 Tbsp sakè**
> **$\frac{1}{4}$ tsp salt**
> **1 Tbsp sesame seeds (you may use ready-toasted varieties)**
> **Ginger pickles *(beni-shōga)***
> **Lemon peel**
> ***Daikon*-radish sprouts**

1. Wash rice till water runs clear. Drain for 20 minutes in a colander.
2. Clean horse mackerel. Wash under running water and dry with paper towels. Sprinkle thoroughly, inside and out, with 1/3 tsp salt. Allow to stand in a colander for 20 minutes.
3. Place horse mackerel on a rack over water, which must not come in contact with the fish, and broil for from 6 to 7 minutes on 1 side. Turn and broil another 6 to 7 minutes on the other side, taking care not to burn. Remove flesh from bones carefully and flake with a fork.
4. In a heavy pot, combine water, sakè, salt, and rice. Cover tightly and, over a medium heat, bring to a boil. Boil for 1 minute. Turn heat to low and cook for another 8 to 9 minutes or until moisture has almost entirely evaporated. Remove from heat and allow to stand, covered, for 10 minutes.
5. Toast sesame seeds (see pp. 104–105). Press as much liquid as possible from ginger pickles. Julienne cut pickles and zest of lemon peel. Cut off and discard bottoms of *daikon*-radish sprouts. Wash and drain. Cut in half if long.
6. Lightly mix flaked mackerel flesh and freshly steamed rice. Mound in individual serving bowls. Sprinkle sesame seeds on top and garnish with *daikon*-radish sprouts and ginger pickles.

Rice with *Wakame* and *Jako* *(Serves 4 to 6)*

The combination of *wakame* and small, calcium-rich, dried white fish or *jako* introduces the fragrance of the sea into your dining room. This amount will serve from 6 to 8 when used as an accompaniment to hearty vegetable dishes.

> **3 cups rice**
> **3 cups water**
> **3 Tbsp and 1 tsp sakè**
> **¼ oz dried *wakame* (further dried in oven and crumbled to make 2 Tbsp)**
> **1 oz (½ cup) *jako***
> **2 Tbsp sesame seeds**
> **4 radishes**

1. Wash rice till water runs clear. Drain for 20 minutes in a colander. In a heavy pot, combine water, 3 Tbsp sakè, and rice. Cover tightly and, over a medium heat, bring to a boil. Boil for 1 minute. Turn heat to low and cook for another 8 to 9 minutes or until moisture has almost entirely evaporated. Remove from heat and allow to stand, covered, for 10 minutes.
2. This recipe calls for rod-shaped dried *wakame*. Dry it for 20 minutes in a slow oven (225°F). Put it in a plastic bag and crush it with a rolling pin.
3. Boil *jako* for a few minutes. Drain in a colander and sprinkle with 1 tsp sakè.
4. Toast sesame seeds (see pp. 104–105). Slice radishes into thin rounds.
5. Quickly mix *jako* and crushed *wakame* with hot steamed rice. Mound in individual serving bowls, sprinkle with toasted sesame seeds, and garnish with radish slices.

Rice with Green Peas, *jako*, and Red Caviar *(Serves 4)*

2¾ cups gultinous rice (or ordinary rice)
3½ cups water
½ tsp salt
1 Tbsp and 1 tsp sakè
¾ cup fresh or frozen green peas
1 oz (½ cup) *jako*
1 oz red caviar

1.   Wash rice in several changes of water till wash water runs clear. Allow to drain in a colander for 20 minutes.
2.   Combine rice, water, salt, and 1 Tbsp sakè in a deep pot with a close-fitting lid. Bring to a boil. Fresh green peas may be added at this point. Frozen green peas should be thawed, parboiled, drained, and folded into rice during the post-cooking steaming period. Cover. Steam over a moderate heat for 3 to 4 minutes. Reduce to low and continue cooking for 7 to 8 minutes. At the end of this period, raise heat to high. Immediately remove from heat and allow to stand, covered, for 10 minutes.
3.   While rice is cooking, parboil *jako* and drain in a colander. Sprinkle with 1 tsp sakè.
4.   Fold *jako* into rice. Heap in individual serving bowls and top with red caviar.

Dried *Sakura* Shrimp and *Wakame* Pilaf *(Serves 4 to 6)*

Feel free to substitute ingredients in this simple, wholesome dish. For instance, frozen mixed vegetables can easily take the place of fresh carrots when you are in a hurry.

6 cups cooked rice (2½ cups before cooking)
¼ cup dried *sakura* shrimp
1½ Tbsp dried, cut *wakame*
3 oz boned chicken meat
⅔ tsp salt
2 oz carrot
¼ cup frozen green peas
3 Tbsp salad oil
Pepper
1 Tbsp sakè or sherry

1.   If cooked rice is unavailable, cook 2 1/2 cups raw, short-grain rice according to instructions on p. 102.
2.   Dice chicken meat and season with salt. Julienne cut carrot. Soften *wakame* in water for 5 minutes. Drain in a colander. Briefly boil frozen green peas; drain them.
3.   In a frying pan, heat salad oil and sauté chicken and carrot. Add cooked rice and continue sautéing over a high heat. Season with salt and pepper.

4.   Add *wakame*, dried shrimp, and green peas. Mix well. Finally, making a well in the middle of the rice to reveal a small area of the frying pan, pour in sakè. Mix well.

Since quantities are large, you may sauté chicken and vegetables half at a time and cook the rice in 2 batches.

Tempura Rice *(Serves 4 to 6)*

This one dish meal consists of tempura served on a bowl of hot rice. Sometimes housewives make more tempura than they need and use the leftovers in this fashion the following day. The recipe calls for fritter-style tempura, but you may substitute medium to large shrimp for a somewhat more luxurious version. In this case, a sprinkling of chopped celery leaves, julienne-cut scallions, or *daikon*-radish sprouts is a tasty addition.

> **6 cups cooked rice (2½ cups before cooking)**
> **Tempura (pp. 77–80) (8 fritters of your choice or leftover tempura of any kind)**
> *Sauce:*
> **1 cup stock (pp. 37–39)**
> **3 Tbsp soy sauce**
> **3 Tbsp sakè**
> **1 Tbsp sugar**

1.   Warm tempura in an oven.
2.   Cut tempura in large bite-size pieces.
3.   Combine sauce ingredients and bring to a boil. Dip tempura in sauce and lift out immediately. Fill individual serving bowls with hot rice. Top with tempura, pour on remaining sauce, and serve hot.

Sashimi Rice *(Serves 4 to 6)*

> **3 cups rice**
> **1 lb tuna sashimi**
> **3 cups and 1 tsp water**
> **3 Tbsp sakè**
> **½ Tbsp *wasabi* horse radish powder**
> **3 Tbsp soy sauce**
> **2 Tbsp sesame seeds**
> **2-in square *nori***
> **3 scallions (white part)**

1.   Wash rice till water runs clear. Drain for 30 minutes in a colander. In a heavy pot, combine 2 cups water, 2 Tbsp sakè, and rice. Cover tightly and, over a medium heat, bring to the boil. Boil for 1 minute. Turn heat to low and cook for another 8 to 9 minutes or until moisture has almost entirely evaporated. Remove from heat and allow to stand, covered, for 10 minutes.

2.   Blend *wasabi* horseradish powder and 1 tsp water. After it has stood long enough for full flavor to develop, combine with 1 Tbsp sakè and soy sauce.

3.   If you are using block sashimi fillet, wash, dry with paper towels, and slice 1/4 in thick. Allow it to stand in *wasabi*-horseradish mixture. Ready sliced sashimi too should be allowed to stand in this mixture.

4.   Toast sesame seeds (see pp. 104–105). Crisp *nori* over an open flame. Put in plastic bag and crumble fairly fine. Julienne cut white parts of scallions fine. Soak in ice water and drain in a colander.

5.   Heap hot rice in deep individual serving bowls, top with tuna sashimi. Sprinkle with sesame seeds and *nori* and top with julienne scallions.

Seafood and Rice *Zōsui* (Serves 4 to 6)

Zōsui means a kind of gruel or soup usually made from cooked rice that has been washed in cold water to eliminate its surface stickiness. Once all the ingredients have been combined, the soup must not be overcooked.

> **4 cups cooked rice (1½ cups before cooking; leftover rice is fine)**
> **16 clams (small)**
> **4 Tbsp sakè**
> **1 squid**
> **8 shrimp**
> **1 tomato (small)**
> **⅓ stalk celery**
> **3 scallions**
> **6 cups chicken broth**
> **1 tsp salt**

1.   Put rice in a colander and wash quickly under running cold water to remove the sticky outer coating on grains. Drain.

2.   Allow clams to stand in salted water in a cool, dark place for from 4 to 5 hours to eject sand. Wash well. Put them in a saucepan, sprinkle with 2 Tbsp sakè, and simmer till they open. Remove clams from pan, reserving liquor. Shell clams and discard shells. Check meat for sand. Gently pour off the top level of the liquor into a separate pan. Discard dregs.

3.   Clean and skin squid (see p. 133). Cut in 1/3-in rings. Devein and shell shrimp, leaving tail-segment shell intact.

4.   Peel and seed tomato and dice fine. Dice celery fine. Slice scallions.

5.   Combine clam liquor with chicken stock, 2 Tbsp sakè, and salt to make 8 cups. Bring to a boil and add rice. Return to boil and add seafood. Simmer for 1 or 2 minutes.

6.   Sprinkle with scallions and serve hot.

Oyster *Zōsui* (Serves 4 to 6)

Elderly people, children, and anyone with a slightly weak stomach will welcome this delicious hot pot, which is low in calories, easy to digest, and rich in taurin (see p. 140).

> 4 cups cooked rice (1½ cups before cooking; leftover rice is fine)
> ⅔ lb oysters
> 1 carrot
> ½ cup *daikon*-radish sprouts (or celery leaves)
> 4 eggs
> 7 cups stock (see pp. 37–39) or chicken broth
> 3 Tbsp sakè
> 1 tsp salt

1. Put rice in a colander and wash quickly under running cold water to remove the sticky outer coating on grains. Drain.
2. Check oysters carefully for bits of shell. Wash and drain in a colander. Cut carrot into thin rounds. Cut off and discard root ends of *daikon*-radish sprouts. Cut in half if long. If using celery leaves, chop. Lightly beat eggs.
3. In a large pot, combine stock, sakè, and salt. Bring to the boil. Add carrot and simmer till crisp-tender. Add rice and return to the boil. Add oysters.
4. Cook oysters about 1 minute. Pour in beaten egg to cover the surface of the liquid. Sprinkle on *daikon*-radish sprouts. Cover. Remove from heat and allow to stand until eggs have cooked to the texture of soft scrambled eggs. Serve in deep bowls.

Crab and Mushroom *Zōsui* (Serves 4)

Easy to digest and warming, this delicately flavored rice soup is just right for busy winter evenings.

> 4 cups cooked rice (1½ cups before cooking; leftover rice is fine)
> ¼ lb crab meat (canned or frozen)
> 8 mushrooms (canned or fresh)
> 4 eggs
> 7 cups stock (see pp. 37–39) or chicken broth
> 1 tsp salt
> ½ cup chopped celery leaves

1. Put rice in a colander and wash quickly under running cold water to remove the sticky outer coating of grains. Drain.
2. Break crab meat apart and check for bony internal membranes. Slice mushrooms. Lightly beat eggs.
3. In a large pot, bring stock and salt to the boil. Add rice and mushrooms. Return to the boil and add crab. Pour in eggs to cover surface of liquid. Sprinkle on celery leaves. Cover. Remove from heat and allow to stand until eggs have cooked to the texture of soft scrambled eggs. Serve hot in individual bowls.

Japanese-style Noodles and Griddle Cakes

Japanese-style Griddle Cake
Okonomi-yaki (p. 114)

The kind of Japanese noodles called *udon* are made from high-gluten wheat, salt, and water. Thoroughly well kneaded dough is rolled thin and cut in long strips. *Udon* may be sold fresh, preboiled, and packaged in vinyl bags or dried in bundles, not unlike spaghetti. The latter is boiled in plenty of water and drained.

Okamè Udon (Serves 4)

Okamè is a word for a woman. In this instance, the round bowl in which the noodles are served represents the facial outline. *Kamaboko* and snowpeas may be used to suggest eyebrows, nose, and mouth.

> **4 packages fresh *udon* noodles (½ lb each)**
> **6 oz chicken thigh meat**
> **4 shrimp**
> **8 pods snow peas**
> **4 slices, ⅓ in thick *kamaboko***
> ***Shichimi* pepper**
> *Broth:*
>   **4½ cups stock**
>   **½ cup sakè**
>   **2 Tbsp soy sauce**
>   **1 tsp salt**

1. Cut chicken into bite-size pieces. Devein shrimp. Boil for 2 minutes in salted water and shell. String snow peas and boil only till crisp-tender.
2. In a saucepan combine stock, sakè, soy sauce, and salt. Bring to a boil, add chicken, and simmer 2 minutes. Skim off scum as it forms.

3.   In a large pot, bring plenty of water to the boil. Drop in noodles. When water boils again, remove from heat. Drain noodles in a colander.

4.   Divide hot noodles among 4 serving bowls. Decorate top with chicken, *kamaoboko* slices, shrimp, and snow peas. Gently pour in broth. A dash of *shichimi* (seven-flavor) pepper adds tantalizing piquancy. People concerned about sodium in the diet should leave the broth.

Wakame Udon *(Serves 4)*

Simple to make, this is a light and refreshing noodle dish.

> **4 packages fresh *udon* noodles ($\frac{1}{2}$ lb each)**
> **2 Tbsp dried, cut *wakame***
> **3 scallions**
> **8 slices, $\frac{1}{3}$ in thick *kamaboko***
> ***Shichimi* pepper**
> **Broth:**
> **$4\frac{1}{2}$ cups stock**
> **$\frac{1}{2}$ cup sakè**
> **2 Tbsp soy sauce**
> **1 tsp salt**

1.   Soften *wakame* in water for 5 minutes. Drain in a colander. Slice scallions in thin rounds. Combine stock, sakè, soy sauce, and salt in a saucepan. Bring to a boil.

2.   In a large pot, bring plenty of water to the boil. Drop noodles in. When water boils again, remove from heat. Drain noodles in a colander.

3.   Divide hot noodles among 4 deep serving bowls. Top with *wakame* and *kamaboko*. Gently pour in broth and sprinkle with scallions. A dash of *shichimi* (seven-flavor) pepper adds tantalizing piquancy. People concerned about sodium in the diet should leave the broth.

Udon Noodles with Fritters *(Serves 4)*

This recipe calls for fritters made of shrimp and celery, which are placed on top of noodles in a lightly flavored broth. Leftover tempura will do just as well.

> **4 packages *udon* noodles ($\frac{1}{2}$ lb each)**
> **$\frac{1}{2}$ lb shrimp**
> **1 Tbsp sakè**
> **$\frac{1}{8}$ tsp salt**
> **1 stalk celery**
> **2 Tbsp flour**
> **Oil for frying**
> ***Shichimi* pepper**

Batter:
  Egg and chilled water to make ½ cup
  ½ cup flour
Broth:
  4½ cups stock
  ½ cup sakè
  2 ½ Tbsp soy sauce
  1 tsp salt
  2 tsp sugar

■ *Fritters*

1.   Devein and shell shrimp. Chop into pieces about the size of an almond. Cut slightly on the diagonal. Sprinkle with sakè and salt and allow to stand 10 minutes. Drain.

2.   Julienne cut celery in pieces about 1 in long. Chop 4 of the best celery leaves. Combine shrimp with celery and celery leaves.

3.   In a measuring cup, lightly beat egg and add chilled water to make ½ cup. Transfer to a bowl. Add flour all at once. Mix lightly with a fork. Ignore small lumps.

4.   In a small bowl, sprinkle 1/2 Tbsp flour over 1/4 shrimp mixture. Add 1/4 batter and mix lightly with fork.

5.   Heat oil to 325°F. Drop batter mix into oil gently. Leave undisturbed for 30 seconds. Then thin the center, which tends to mound, with a fork. Fry till crisp—from 2 to 3 minutes, turning once or twice. Repeat these processes with remaining fritter ingredients. Drain fritters as they are fried.

■ *Udon noodles*

1.   Combine stock, sakè, soy sauce, salt, and sugar in a saucepan and bring to a boil. Remove from heat.

2.   In a large pot, bring plenty of water to the boil. Drop in noodles. When water boils again, remove from heat. Drain noodles in a colander.

3.   Divide the hot noodles among 4 deep serving bowls. Top each serving with a fritter and gently pour in the broth. Serve at once with *shichimi* pepper. People concerned about too much sodium in the diet may eat the noodles and fritter and leave the broth.

This dish is good made with buckwheat noodles (*soba*) as well. Cook it according to package directions. If you use leftover tempura, heat it in an oven.

Japanese-style Griddle Cake *Okonomi-yaki* (*12 5-in griddle cakes*)

These griddle cakes, made with something like Western pancake batter, are topped with all kinds of vegetable or seafood. Family and friends frequently enjoy cooking and eating them together in a relaxed atmosphere of fun and companionship.
Use whatever ingredients you have on hand. Fish and meat should be cut small and sautéed before being added to the batter.

½ lb cabbage
4 oz white-flesh fish fillet
Salt
Pepper
Salad oil
4 scallions
¼ cup frozen corn
4 slices ham
½ cup dried *sakura* shrimp
Worcestershire sauce
Powdered seaweed *aonori*
Ketchup
Mayonnaise
Batter:
2 eggs and water to make 2 cups
3 cups flour
¾ cup milk

1.   Lightly beat eggs and combine with water to make 2 cups. Add flour and milk. Mix with a rotary egg beater.
2.   Shred cabbage. Skin and bone fish, cut into bite-size pieces, sprinkle with salt and pepper, and sauté on both sides in hot salad oil. Cut scallions into thin rounds. Briefly boil, then drain, frozen corn. Julienne cut ham.
3.   Heat and oil griddle or frying pan. Combine batter with ham, fish, vegetables, and dried shrimp. Pour 1/12 of this mixture on the griddle. Bake on one side. Turn and bake till done. Continue with the remaining batter.

Eat these griddle cakes with Worcestershire sauce and *aonori* or with ketchup or mayonnaise or a mixture of these dressings. The following are suggestions for other ingredients that make delicious *okonomi-yaki*: *wakame* (softened and squeezed to remove moisture), *jako*, frozen asparagus (sauté before using), mushrooms, sweet green peppers, beef, pork, crisp-fried bacon, mozzarella cheese, bananas, kiwi fruit.

Jako Potato Pancakes *(Serves 4)*

Jako, or sardine fry, may be either well dried or partially dried. The latter variety is called for in this dish.

2 oz (1 cup) *jako*
2 rashers bacon
2 cups grated raw potato
3 Tbsp milk
1 egg
¼ cup flour
¼ tsp baking powder
1 Tbsp grated onion

1 tsp salt
Salad oil

1. Pour boiling water over *jako*. Drain. Sauté bacon till crisp; crumble it.
2. Mix grated potato and milk in a bowl. Add lightly beaten egg and all other ingredients, except salad oil, and mix.
3. Heat salad oil in a frying pan. Dropping mixture into the pan with a spoon, fry small pancakes till they are golden brown on both sides.

Ingredients

Fish

Bonito *(Katsuo)*
A variety of tuna, the highly migratory bonito lives in warm water and weighs from 1 1/2 to 5 pounds. Its meat is firm in texture, and its oil is neutral. It is suitable for baking, broiling, and grilling.

Cod *(Tara)*
Although size varies with species, in general cod weighs between 2 1/2 and 25 pounds. Its white flesh is lightly flavored and low in oil. Good baked or broiled or in soup, it is marketed fresh, salted, smoked, and filleted. Though similar to it, haddock, which is considered tastier, is more expensive.

Flatfishes: Halibut, Flounder, Sole, Turbot *(Hirame, Karei, Shita-birame)*
There are many varieties of these delicately flavored fishes, most of which are prized. They range in size from 1/4 of a pound to about 10 pounds. Often what appears as "fillet of sole Meunière" on menus is actually fillet of flounder, because true sole are no longer imported from England and Belgium. Cooking methods are the same for all of these fishes.

Horse Mackerel *(Aji)*
Low in fat and pleasantly flavored, this very popular fish is only about 1 foot in length. It is delicious poached, steamed, baked, broiled, or sautéed.

Mackerel *(Saba)*
High in oil, mackerel occur in many different varieties and range in size from 1/2 to 30 pounds. They prefer coastal waters, where they migrate after schools of sardines. Especially rich in EPA (see pp. 139–140), mackerel in the diet helps prevent arteriosclerosis and cardiac infarction. Since it contains more histamines than other fish, however, it can be a problem for people with allergies.

Orange Roughy
After appearing on the American market in 1979, this reddish-orange fish from the Tasman Sea off New Zealand began to sell very well. Filleted, its white flesh lends itself to many different methods of preparation and holds its shape well.

Red Sea Bream *(Tai)*
This delicately fragrant fish, which has little oil, is best prepared simply: broiled, pan-fried, or grilled with melted butter. Because of its blandness, it is good in soups and stews. In New Zealand, the same fish is called red snapper.

Salmon *(Sakè)*

Salmon is loved all over the world and apparently has been for a very long time, judging by the pictures of the fish found carved on ancient reindeer bones in the Pyrenees of southern France. These pictures of salmon swimming in rivers in glacial regions indicate that knowledge of the fish dates far back into history.

The flesh of some salmon is a paler red than that of others. The difference is one of pigmentation and has nothing to do with nutritional value.

As is well known, salmon return to spawn in the streams of their own origins. Once they enter these rivers, they must swim upstream and, since they eat nothing, grow thin. The flesh of fish in this state is not good to eat. Consequently, salmon are usually caught in the sea before they head inland. This very delicious fish lends itself to many different cooking methods, including poaching, steaming, baking, frying, grilling, and broiling.

Chinook, or king salmon, is a large fish, the tender flesh of which is rich in oil and ranges in color between white and red. It is extremely good smoked. Coho, or silver salmon, is a pink-flesh fish often sold canned. Sockeye, or red salmon, has firm flesh of a beautiful deep red color. Chum is the least oily of the salmon varieties. Its flesh is pale in color. Pink salmon is the smallest. With flesh ranging from pale to deep pink, this fish accounts for half of the canned salmon produced in America.

Swordfish *(Mekajiki)*

Wild and bold in disposition, the large (4 yards and from 100 to 200 pounds) swordfish will attack other big fish and even whales. Distributed throughout the seas of the world, it is migratory and tropical in nature. The flesh, which is off-white in color, has a low oil content. It is good broiled and grilled and benefits from being served with some kind of sauce.

Tuna *(Maguro)*

The tuna is a large migratory inhabitant of the upper levels of the ocean. When cooked, the pale pink flesh of the tuna resembles chicken in flavor and is widely sold canned. Like the bonito and sardines, much of the flesh of the bluefin tuna, which may weigh as much as a thousand pounds, is bloody in color, a trait that some people find unpleasant. Nonetheless, this part of the fish is high in non-saturated fats, iron, and vitamins A and D and the B-group vitamins. In fact, it has twice as much iron as other parts of the flesh. Furthermore, the iron is in an easily absorbable state.

White Sea Bass *(Suzuki)*

With its elegant and delicious flavor, sea bass, which may weigh from 10 to 40 pounds, lends itself to many cooking methods and is sold whole, dressed, filleted, cut in steaks, or smoked.

Crustaceans and Shellfish

Clams *(Hamaguri)*

This most representative of the bivalves comes in several size varieties, the larger ones generally being the tougher. Small little-neck clams may be eaten raw. Medium-size cherry-stone clams may be eaten raw or baked. Larger clams find their ways into various cooked foods, including chowders. Succinic acid determines the flavor of clams, which are rich in taurin and vitamins A and B_2. The taurin in clams, like that in oysters and scallops, helps prevent cardiac illness.

Use only live clams. Check them to see that the shells are closed, and discard any that are, and remain, slightly open. Healthy clams make a clear sound when tapped together.

Crabs *(Kani)*

With their delicate flavor, beautiful color, and arresting shapes, crabs add great distinction to the table. They may be purchased live, frozen, or canned and may be used in a wide variety of cold and hot dishes. As highly prized as shrimp and lobster, the blue crab is immediately recognizable for its pointed ovate body and its blue coloration. Soft-shell crabs—crabs that have recently shed their shells and have not had time for their new ones to harden—are a great delicacy deep-fried and served with lemon. Crabs that are about to shed are identifiable by small spots on their rear legs. People fortunate enough to catch them store such crabs in aquariums until they shed. Blue crabs are boiled in salted water for from 10 to 20 minutes. They are next plunged in cold water and drained. Then the meat is picked from the shells.

Dungeness crabs are a splendid bright red when boiled. They weigh from 1 3/4 to 4 pounds, of which about 25 percent is edible. They are cooked the same way as blue crabs are.

King crabs may weigh as much as 10 lbs. Cooked, their meat is a stunning white trimmed with bright red. It is delicious and correspondingly expensive. Cooked, frozen leg and body meat are sold separately.

Although in the past, crab meat has been criticized for its high cholesterol content, it has recently been discovered to contain taurin content (less than oysters), the effects of which manifest themselves over an extended period.

Oysters *(Kaki)*

People all over the world are so fond of them that oysters are often referred to as the queen of the sea. Glycogen accounts for their flavor and may reach as much as 5 percent of their total volume in winter. This glycogen is in an easily assimilable form and serves as an immediate supply of energy. In addition, oysters are rich in vitamins and such minerals as zinc, copper, and iron, all of which are lacking in the modern diet of processed foods like bread made from bleached flour.

Glycine, a simple amino acid, together with glycogen, makes oysters delicious. Lemon, reacting with glycine, further enhances their flavor.

There seems to be no foundation for the idea that during the period between May and August (months in the names of which the letter *r* does not appear), when they reproduce, oysters contain harmful substances. Apparently the truth is that, during reproduction time the level of nutrients in the oyster's body drops, correspondingly lowering the levels of glycogen and glycine content.

Eat raw oysters very fresh. Even refrigerated, they lose flavor fast. The best way is to shell them, sprinkle a few drops of lemon juice on them, and eat them together with their own liquor. Lemon cuts odors and accents flavors.

Scallops *(Hotate-gai)*

The lovely form of the scallop shell has been a favorite artistic and architectural motif for centuries. Taken from the sea and put in a quiet place, scallops will open their shells to about 30 degrees but snap them shut again at the first sign of something untoward. Scallops that behave in this way are in good condition. Since, unlike other bivalves, scallops cannot close their shells tight, they rapidly lose liquid upon being taken from the water. The part usually eaten is the large adductor muscle that holds the shells together. In areas where they are produced, scallops are harvested, shelled, and immediately frozen. They keep their flavors well frozen. They are rich in protein and have a high succinic-acid content. Scallops are best prepared in simple ways.

Shrimp *(Ebi)*

Throughout the world there are hundreds of different species of this universally popular crustacean. Delicate flavor plus firm texture are two of their great attractions. Others are the ease and speed with which they can be prepared and the splendor they bring to the dining table.

Usually they are categorized by size; that is, how many make a pound—16–20, extra large; 21–30, large; and 31–40, medium. Generally speaking, 2 pounds of raw shrimp will produce 1 pound after shelling and deveining. Even marine biologists hesitate to make definite statements about the distinction between shrimp and prawn. In America, *shrimp* is the accepted word. The British refer to anything about 2 or 2 1/2 inches in length as a shrimp; anything larger they call a prawn. *Scampi* is the plural of the Italian word *scampo*, a large greenish prawn.

Edible Seaweeds and Dried Foods

Traditionally the Japanese people have liked seaweeds and have believed them valuable in the preservation of good health. Recent research had reinforced this belief by showing that seaweeds are rich in kalium, calcium, iron, and iodine and in vegetable fibers, which are thought to be important in cancer prevention. Moreover, the alginic acid found in seaweeds helps prevent hypertension. The following are the most popular kinds of seaweed products.

Aonori

A beautiful color, this powdery seaweed is fragrant and has a refreshing piquancy. It is usually sold in bottles or bags.

Hijiki

Hijiki, which occur in most Japanese waters, may be simply sun dried or steamed and then dried. In either case, better quality products are thoroughly dry and evenly colored. After being softened in lukewarm water for 20 minutes, they may be sautéed, simmered, or used in salads. They retain their dark blackish color after being softened.

Kombu

Kombu is most often used, sometimes alone but generally with flakes of dried bonito, in preparing fragrant, delicious Japanese-style stock. The thicker *kombu* is, the more expensive it is. The best comes from the waters off such places as Rausu, Rijiri, and Hidaka on the northern island of Hokkaido.

Glutamic acid in *kombu* combined with inosinic acid in dried bonito account for the fine flavor these ingredients impart to stocks. *Kombu* contains from 20 to 60 percent more iodine than *wakame*.

Nori

The seaweed known as *nori* is gathered and dried into rectangular, paper-thin sheets, sold in bundles of 6 to 10 sheets. The annual Japanese consumption of *nori* is enormous: 9 billion sheets, or roughly 80 sheets per person. It is rich in minerals; vegetable fibers; and such vitamins as A, which is thought to help prevent cancer formation and to hinder the development of colds; vitamin C; and vitamins B_1 and B_2. It is a good idea to eat a small amount of *nori* regularly.

Nori is generally very lightly toasted before eating. Two sheets are held together and moved slowly back and forth over a direct flame for a very short time. Toasting intensifies the aroma. The seaweed is then used to wrap some kinds of sushi (*makizushi*) or *omusubi*, patties of cooked rice usually containing pickles or fish and very popular for picnics and lunch boxes.

Nori sold pretoasted and flavored with soy sauce is widely used. It may be wrapped around cheese, butter, or *kamaboko* for tasty hors d'oeuvres.

Wakame

Found in the seas all around the Japanese islands, *wakame* is marketed in the following forms and is used in soups, salads, and hors d'oeuvres.

A.   *Dried* wakame

Softened in cold or lukewarm water for 5 minutes, this naturally dried product expands to from 8 to 10 times its original volume. Washed thoroughly, drained, dipped into boiling water, and then plunged into cold water, it assumes a beautiful green color. Before it may be used in cooking, it must be trimmed of hard sections.

Since it is better still slightly crisp, if you intend to use it in soups, which require further cooking, shorten the initial softening period. Cut it into bite-size pieces before adding it to the soup for no more than a final heating. You may soften a large batch of *wakame*, divide it into convenient quantities, and freeze them. Use the water in which seaweeds are softened for cooking because it is rich in minerals.

B.   *Boiled and salted* wakame

Wakame taken from the sea is briefly boiled, cooled in water, drained, and sprinkled with coarse salt. It is usually sold in plastic bags. The hard parts of the seaweed are cut away in the preparation process. Furthermore, since it has not been subjected to drying, it requires only washing to be ready for use. Wash it several times to remove all salt and drain it well. Cut it into bite-size pieces for use in soups and salads. This variety too may be washed in large batches, which may then be subdivided for freezing.

C.   *Dried, cut* wakame

Cut fine, this kind of *wakame* is sold in small packages. *Wakame* is briefly boiled, drained, and salted. The salt causes dehydration. The tough stalks are removed, and the salt is washed out. Then, the *wakame* is cut into small pieces and dried in hot air currents.

Because it has already been cooked and desalinated, this most convenient form of *wakame* needs only to be softened in water for a few minutes. During softening, 1/4 oz expands 17 times to 4 oz.

Dried bonito flakes *(Kezuribushi)*

It is said that fillets of bonito steamed and dried to considerable hardness were originally used as portable foodstuff by soldiers on campaign. Today, however, dried bonito is most widely employed in preparing Japanese-style stock.

Bonito swim upward into Japanese waters in the spring. For drying, they must have just the right amount of fat. The process, including steaming, drying, and stimulating the formation of mold on the fillets, requires about 3 months.

In the past, dried bonito fillets were customarily given as gifts on occasions demanding congratulations. But this practice has gradually died out since shaving the hard fillets is time- and labor-consuming and requires a special planelike tool.

Instead of shaving their own bonito, most housewives today prefer to buy it preshaved in large bags or in small packages containing individual servings. Although less fragrant than hand-shaved bonito, these preparation have the virtue of convenience. In addition to use in stock, bonito flakes are sprinkled, as they are, on boiled, chilled spinach and on tofu. In addition to inosinic acid, bonito contains more than 200 elements contributing to its distinctive aroma.

Harusame

This vermicellilike product made from starch is used in one-dish casserole meals and salads. Though nothing definite is known about its derivation, the romantic name *harusame*, or spring rain, is thought to have arisen from the rainlike appearance of the noodles as they are hung for final drying. Originally they were made of the starch left when protein is extracted from green soybeans that have been allowed to soak in water. Today, however, starch from white potatoes or sweet potatoes is more widely used. Unlike those made from bean starch, *harusame* made of potato starch disintegrate if simmered long. Soak them for a short time in water, dip them in boiling water, and drain them quickly.

Fish-based Products

To produce these various processed foods, white-flesh fish (cod, shark, and so on) is soaked in water, salted, mixed with starch and seasonings, and pounded to a paste. Before cooking, the paste is formed in various ways: *kamaboko, chikuwa, hanpen, tsumirè, satsuma-agè,* crab-flavored *kamaboko,* and so on. All of these foods must be refrigerated and eaten within the period specified on the wrapper.

Kamaboko
Considered high quality, *kamaboko* is made by mounding fish paste on a small board and steaming or baking it. It may be eaten as it is and has a resilient texture. The outside of some *kamaboko* is dyed pink—this has no effect on the flavor—for use in conjunction with white on auspicious occasions. In Japan, red (or pink) and white are the colors of congratulations.

Chikuwa
A somewhat lower-grade food than *kamaboko, chikuwa* was originally produced by coating lengths of bamboo with fish paste, steaming or roasting it, and removing the bamboo to form cylinders. Flavor and aroma improve if *chikuwa* is roasted.

Hanpen
About 1/2 in thick, soft cushion-shaped *hanpen* is made by steaming a mixture of fish paste and starch. It is cut and used in miso soups.

Tsumirè and satsuma-agè
Both are used in casserole cooking. *Tsumirè* are balls of fish paste boiled, and *satsuma-agè* are fish paste worked into various shapes and deep-fried.

Crab-flavored kamaboko
Containing no crab at all, this very popular product is shaped and dyed to look like crab leg meat, which it resembles in flavor and texture. It is an attractive addition to salads.

Vegetables

Burdock (Gobō)
The Chinese used this popular root vegetable as a medical treatment for dropsy and constipation and as an antidote. Scrape away the skin with the back of a

kitchen knife and allow the burdock to stand in water for a while to eliminate some of its characteristic astringency.

Chinese cabbage *(Hakusai)*
Indispensable for winter casserole dishes, Chinese cabbage has tender leaves with thick central spines, which are tenderized by cooking. It may be sliced and eaten raw in salads. In the past, mounds of heads of Chinese cabbage in cord-bound bundles standing in front of green grocers signaled the approach of winter. Housewives purchased this vegetable to make pickles, spiced with red chili pepper, that would be eaten by the whole family throughout the cold months. Today, since few families make their own pickles, one whole head of Chinese cabbage is considered too much; and the vegetable is sold cut in half, or even quartered, and packaged in plastic wrap.

Select Chinese cabbage that is very white and firmly headed. Black spots on the stalks indicate illness. Although not harmful to human beings, Chinese cabbage displaying these spots is unpleasant to look at. This vegetable stores fairly well. Use outer leaves first. Wrap remainder in paper and store in a cool place.

Cucumbers *(Kyūri)*
Although actually a summer vegetable, cucumbers are now available year round. The Japanese version is more slender than the Western cucumber, and its skin is so thin that peeling is unnecessary. Select dark green cucumbers with pointed bumps on the skin. Cut off the ends and scrape away the bumps with a knife before slicing. They are delicious chilled and served with a dip.

Daikon radish
The *daikon* radish, said to have originated in the region extending from the Caucasus to Greece, is the most widely used of all vegetables in Japan. From the beginning of the ninth century, it was included among the seven medicinal herbs eaten with rice gruel at the beginning of the New Year. It has long been known to contain vitamin C and the digestive enzyme diastase, and recently its dietary-fiber content has become a topic of interest. In December, a temple called Ryōtoku-ji in Kyoto distributes boiled *daikon* to worshippers. Anyone who eats this *daikon* is supposed to be ensured longevity and freedom from palsy.

Daikon-radish sprouts *(Kaiware-na)*
When radish seeds have germinated and have grown 2 leaves, the sprouts are harvested. Charming in appearance, these sprouts add color and peppery zest to salads and other dishes.

Devil's tongue jelly *(Konnyaku)*
In very ancient times, the tuber from which this jelly is made was regarded as medicine: it was not until the sixth century that it began to be eaten. Sliced and dried, the tuber is ground in a mortar. The heavy residue at the bottom of the mortar is collected and treated with milk of lime to cause it to congeal. Parboil *konnyaku* before eating it.

125

Eggplant *(Nasu)*
Japanese eggplants are small and delicious in their entirety. They go well with oil and therefore make delicious sautées and tempura. Choose eggplant that are blackish purple, shiny, and resilient and that have a whitish demarcation zone between the body and the calyx.

Enoki **mushrooms**
These creamy-white, slender mushrooms (about 5 in long) are used in casserole dinners and soups. To raise them, spores are sown in sterilized bottles containing sawdust, rice bran, and slaked lime. The mushrooms are usually sold in plastic bags. Always discard the root ends. When dark yellow and sticky, they are too old to eat.

Kabocha **squash**
The name *kabocha* is supposed to derive from Cambodia, from which the vegetable is said to have been introduced into Japan. The skin of this squash is dark green, and the flesh orange with a dense texture. Eaten in the winter, it is supposed to protect from palsy and colds and to ward off evil.

Scallions *(Negi)*
Actually the Japanese *negi* or *naga-negi* is somewhat larger than the Western scallion. In general the tough, unpleasantly flavored green part is discarded. Be on guard for dirt in the region where green shades into white. The white part of the Japanese *negi* is used as is the white part of the scallion.

Shiitake **mushrooms**
This mushroom is found in nature on a kind of oak called *shii*, or chinquapin. For commercial production, oak logs are inoculated with mushroom spores. Tough, inedible *shiitake* stems are cut off and discarded. Only the cap is used. Wash quickly from the upper side only, without allowing water to reach the spongy underside. Good *shiitake* have thick, rounded caps. Thin, broken, or discolored caps are of poor quality, as are those with blackish undersides. *Shiitake* may be used in any of the ways in which you would use champignons.

Snow Peas *(Sayaendō)*
These immature pea pods are delicious briefly boiled, cooled, and added to salads. They give both color and fragrance to soups. Sautéed in oil or butter they are a very attractive side vegetable. Remember to string them before boiling them.

Tofu (Bean curd)

Sometimes called the meat of the field, tofu, made from soybeans, contains 7 percent vegetable protein, which presents no cause for concern in connection with cholesterol. To make tofu, soybeans are soaked in water to soften and ground to produce soy milk, which must be separated from the pulp residue, called *okara*.

At present, *okara* is little used for food, although it can be quite delicious cooked with vegetables and seasoned with soy sauce and sugar. A coagulant called *nigari* is added to soy milk to make tofu, which may be of 2 general types: cotton (*momen*) and silk (*kinu*). To make cotton tofu, perforated forms are lined with cotton cloth; and the mixture of soy milk and coagulant is flushed into the form. Liquid seeps out through the cotton and the holes in the form, resulting in a fairly firm tofu. Silk tofu is made by pouring soy milk and coagulant into forms without holes. It sets to a texture that is figuratively as smooth as silk.

When purchasing, make sure the tofu is white and unbroken and kept in clean water. Examine the production date on packaged tofu; purchase none that is more than 5 to 7 days old. Store leftover tofu, in water, in the refrigerator. Changing the water daily extends the duration of the period during which tofu may be kept.

Although tofu was introduced from China, the Japanese evolved a version suited to their own tastes. Japanese tofu is more tender and delicate in flavor and is sold in somewhat larger blocks than Chinese tofu. *Tofu* in this book always refers to cotton tofu, though feel free to use silk tofu in soups if you prefer it.

Seasonings and Spices

Garlic *(Ninniku)*
This pungent bulb, often crushed or diced fine and sautéed in oil as a seasoning, masks odors as well as adding its own distinctive flavor. Since it burns easily, begin sautéing with a low heat and increase to a medium heat.

Ginger *(Shōga)*
The rhizome of the ginger plant, peeled and sliced, unpeeled and ground, or ground and squeezed to produce juice, is employed in various foods for its high fragrance and considerable pungency. It is especially important in masking fish odors. Sliced and pickled in a sweet-and-sour vinegar mixture, it is an excellent accompaniment to roast fish and an indispensable garnish for sushi. In addition to the flavor emphasis it gives, ginger aids digestion.

Mirin
This distinctively Japanese seasoning is produced by adding rice mold and steamed glutinous rice to sakè and allowing the mixture to ferment. The starch is saccharized in the process, and a liquor that is 42 percent sugars and 14 percent alcohol results. The addition of a small amount of *mirin* to the marinade for *teriyaki* mellows flavors and heightens the gloss of the glaze. A tablespoon of *mirin* has the sweetening power of a teaspoon of sugar.

Miso (Bean paste)
Miso is made by fermenting steamed soybeans to which have been added rice mold, salt, and water. The mixture is reduced to a paste form and, today, usually sold in plastic bags. Of the many different varieties, the darkest ones have the

strongest and saltiest taste. Paler versions are lighter and less salty. The milder ones are more widely used. Combining different varieties gives deeper, richer flavors. Each 3 ounces of the dark variety, usually called *akamiso*, or red miso, contains 0.42 ounce of salt. The lighter varieties contains 0.37 ounce of salt per 3 ounces. This means that a tablespoon contains 0.08 ounce. Store in a cool place.

Red chili pepper *(Aka tōgarashi)*

It is often said that, in the case of peppers, the smaller, the hotter. This small (2 in long) red pepper is generally sold dried and packaged. Soften it for a few minutes in cold or lukewarm water before seeding and using either whole or cut into thin rings. Owing to its shape, this pepper is referred to as an eagle's talon. Both the pepper and dishes containing it are known as *namban*, or Southern Barbarian, because it was first introduced into Japan, in about the seventeenth century, by the Portuguese and Spanish, whom the Japanese called by this less than flattering term. Although there is no definite proof, it appears from archaeological evidence that the red pepper originated in central Mexico, from which it traveled north. Columbus took it to Spain, and from there it made its way to England and ultimately to Japan.

Sakè

Sakè—second-grade is fine for cooking—is added to simmered foods and used as a tenderizer for fish and shellfish. A sprinkling of sakè on roasted and broiled foods brings out finer flavors. Furthermore, flavors are enhanced and odors are masked when a small amount is added to dishes like Rice with Horse Mackerel (p. 106). Sherry is suggested as a possible substitute, but every effort should be made to procure real sakè.

Sesame oil

Sometimes this fragrant oil, pressed from sesame seeds, is added in small quantities to the oil in which tempura is fried. A little of it introduced at the final stage of cooking of sautées and other foods, adds fragrance to stimulate the appetite. Think of it more as a seasoning than as an ordinary oil and store it in the refrigerator to prevent oxidation.

Sesame seeds *(Goma)*

Peoples of the Middle East and Asia have loved sesame for centuries. Toasted and ground or chopped, the seeds have a delightful, appetite-stimulating aroma. Oil pressed from sesame seeds helps lower blood-cholesterol levels. Sesame seeds are sold whole and raw, ground, toasted, or hulled or in pastes like tahini. Whole seeds must be toasted to stimulate emergence of fragrance. It is convenient to toast them in quantity and store them in tightly lidded bottles. They are easier to digest and assimilate if chopped or ground. Like soybeans, sesame seeds have played a vital part in the wholesome nutrition of Chinese and Japanese Buddhist priests who, in the past, were restricted to vegetarian diets. Even today, Japanese Buddhist temples serve vegetarian meals (*shōjin ryōri*) that include a tofu made from sesame. See pp. 104–105 for instructions on toasting sesame seeds.

Shichimi *tōgarashi* (Seven-flavor condiment)

This combination of chopped red chili pepper, *sanshō* pepper, flax seed, poppy seed, sesame seed, and dried orange peel adds fragrance and piquancy to many different kinds of foods, especially *udon* noodles. Store in the refrigerator.

Soy sauce *(Shōyu)*

Like miso, one of the most important seasonings used in Japanese cooking, soy sauce is made from steamed (generally pressed) soybeans and toasted wheat to which a fermentation mold called *kōji* is added. After further additions of water and salt, the mash is allowed to ferment. Finally it is pasteurized, and the sauce is separated from the residue.

Soy sauce may be light or dark in color. The dark variety is more generally used and therefore accounts for the bulk of production. The slightly saltier light variety is preferred when darkening of food colors is undesirable. Three ounces of dark soy sauce contain 0.48 ounce of salt. This means that a tablespoon contains 0.09 ounce. In this book, *soy sauce* always means the dark kind. Store soy sauce in a cool, dark place.

Vinegar *(Su)*

Japanese vinegars may be fermented, synthetic, or a combination of the two. Delicately flavored, fermented rice vinegars are favored for such traditional foods as sushi. Synthetic vinegars are produced by thinning acetic acid with water and adding salt, sweeteners, and chemical seasonings. To improve its quality, this synthetic product is often mixed with fermented vinegar. All three of these vinegar types are milder than cider or wine vinegar. A tart sauce called *ponzu* for use with casserole dinners is often made by combining citrus (lemon, for instance) juice with soy sauce. If rice vinegar is unavailable, substitute cider vinegar to which you have added small amounts of sugar and white wine.

Wasabi horseradish

Good quality *wasabi* is cultivated beside cold, clear, mountain streams brimming with water from thawing snows. The root is ground to use as a spicy condiment in several kinds of food, but most notably with sashimi and sushi. Since fresh *wasabi* is virtually unobtainable outside Japan, you must substitute a powdered variety or prepared *wasabi* paste in tubes sold in most stores specializing in oriental foods. The powder, which is actually made from white Western horseradish, must be mixed to a smooth paste with a small amount of water and allowed to stand until full flavor develops. It may be frozen.

About Fish as Food

Freshness

Whole Fish
Judging freshness of whole fish is easy: first look at the eyes. If they are clear and full, the fish is fresh. They become cloudy and sink inward as time passes. The gills are pink when the fish is fresh and later begin turning gray. In fresh fish, the belly is lustrous and resilient. Later it grows dull and loses resiliency. In fish that are not of first freshness, scales begin falling off.

Fillets, Slices, and Steaks
Judgment is a little more difficult in these cases. As time passes, blood and fluids emerge from cut fish to collect in the wrapped containers in which markets display them. A great deal of such fluid indicates passage of considerable time, as does a brownish instead of a red color. Sliced fish that feels slimy to the touch is likely to be fairly old. But, since in most instances you will not be allowed to touch it directly, it is a good idea to ask sales personnel about freshness and determine whether the fish is fresh enough to eat raw or must be cooked.

Frozen Fish
Examine dates on packaging.

Sprinkling Fish with Salt
Salt is sprinkled on fish, which is then allowed to stand for a while in a colander, in order to stimulate the elimination of odor-causing elements. The fish is then wiped clean to minimize odor. In addition, salting firms the flesh of very tender fish.

Cleaning
Fresh fish and shellfish must be first washed. This is true of sliced fish as well. Then they must be dried with paper towels. Removing viscera and gills keeps whole fish fresh longer.

Filleting

The process of cutting a whole fish into two fillets and the central bone section is basic to all other preparations.
1.   Scale the fish. Less mess from flying scales results if the fish is held in a paper bag or wrapped in newspaper during this step.
2.   Position the fish on a cutting board with the belly toward you and the head

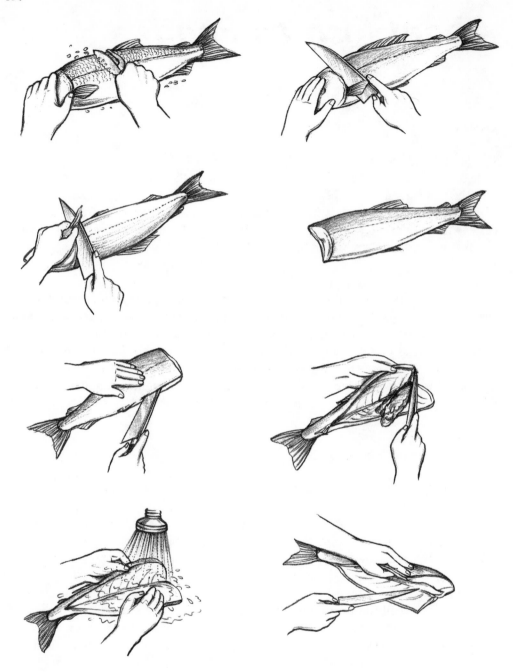

on your left. Insert your knife behind the gills and cut to the back bone. Turn the fish and repeat this incision to sever the head from the body.

3.   Make an incision in the belly from the point where the head was cut off to the ventral fin. Scrape out viscera with knife point.

4.   Wash well in running water. Cut along the lower edge of the central bone to facilitate removal of blood vessels during washing.

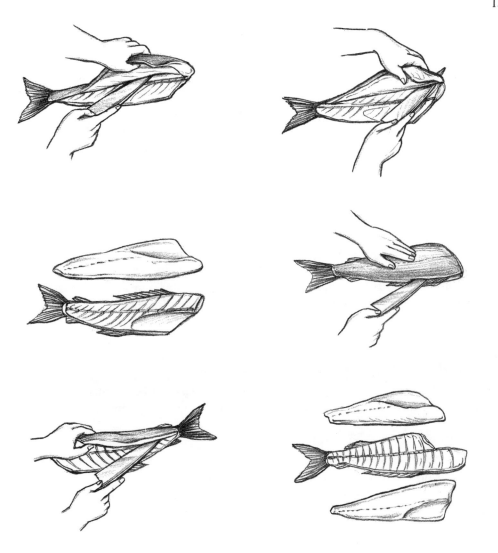

5. With the belly toward you and the tail on your left, hold the upper part of the fish with your left hand. Starting at the head end, cut the lower side of the upper fillet free from the bones. Your knife should move along the spine as you continue to cut all the way to the tail.

6. Next, drawing the knife toward you, beginning at the head end and working toward the tail, cut the upper side of the fillet from the bones. Lift the fillet as you cut. This frees the whole, boneless fillet from the skeleton.

7. Now turn the fish so that the dorsal (back) fin is toward you and the tail is on your left. Working from the head end and moving the tip of the knife along the spine, cut from the head to the tail.

8. Turn the fish so that the belly is toward you and the tail is on your right. Running the tip of the knife along the spine, cut from the tail to the head to free the fillet from the bones.

Removing Gills and Viscera

This step is necessary when fish is being prepared whole, as in the case of fried sea bream.

1.   Scale the fish. Use a scaler, or the back of the tip of the knife, and work from the tail toward the head.

2.   First make an incision under the jaw. Then make an incision from the jaw to the tail running down the ventral fin. The gills and viscera may then be removed without breakage.

3.   Wash under running water. Use the tip of the knife to cut along the central bone in order to facilitate removal of blood vessels. Dry well.

Shellfish

Sand

Clams and similar bivalves frequently contain sand. To stimulate them to eject it, after washing the shells thoroughly, allow the clams to stand in salted water (1 Tbsp salt to each quart of water) in a cool, dark place for half a day. It is better not to refrigerate.

   After they have ejected sand, wash them again. If the clams are to be preboiled for use in soups, when they have opened their shells, check for sand. Wash them gently in the broth in which they were boiled. Strain this through cheesecloth before adding to soups or other foods. Remember always to add clams and other shellfish late in the cooking process. Overexposure to heat toughens them.

Storing

If possible, eat shellfish on the day in which they are purchased. When they must be kept over till the next day, first wash them thoroughly under running water. The *enteritis vibrio* that tends to infect seafood is highly intolerant of fresh water. Place the shellfish in a low, flat pan and cover with wet paper towels. Store refrigerated at about 12°F.

Oysters

Shucked oysters must be checked for persisting bits of shell. Next wash them in salted water (1 Tbsp salt to each quart of water). Place a colander in a large bowl. Wash them under running water, shaking the colander all the while. Change water and wash again, shaking the colander. Drain. They are now ready for use.

Shrimp

1.   Wash and dry shrimp. Bending the body, insert a sharp-pointed skewer (preferably a bamboo skewer) between shell segments and pull out the intestinal tract. This process is referred to as deveining.

2.   Leaving the tail-shell and one last segment intact, shell the shrimp. Do not wash again.

3.   Trim the tail-segment shell as shown.

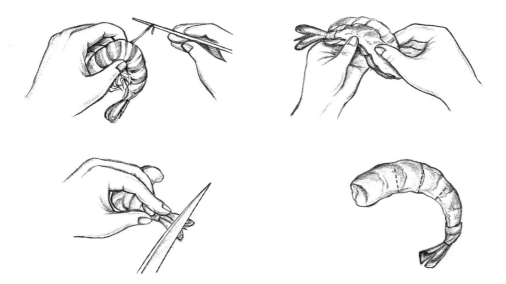

4. To prevent curling during frying, make incisions in the underside of the body at 1/3-in intervals. The incisions should penetrate to about 2/3 the thickness of the body.

Squid

1. Insert your finger inside the body cavity and sever the ligament connecting the viscera and the body.
2. Remove viscera by pulling tentacles. Remove internal cartilage.
3. Insert your finger into the trunk and pull off the tail fin.
4. Grip the outer skin. A paper towel makes it easier to hold.
5. Skin by pulling.
6. Open the body into a single sheet by slitting from inside.
7. An additional thin skin remains on both sides of the flesh. Pull this off. It is unpleasant to chew and causes frying oil to spatter.

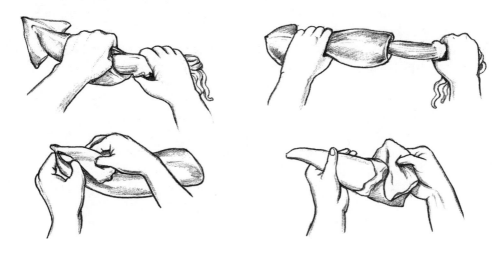

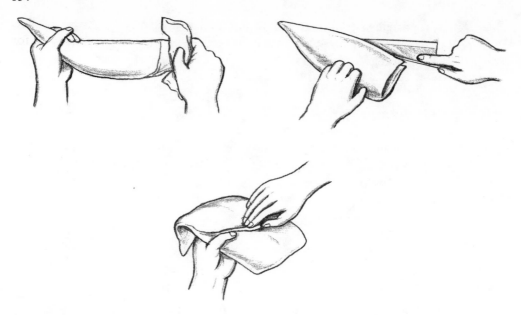

Thawing Frozen Fish

To thaw frozen fish in such a way as to return them as close as possible to original condition the following points are important. Low temperatures and an extended thawing period are best. It is possible to thaw faster by putting seafoods in warm water or a warm place; but, if you adopt these courses, you must expect loss in quality.

Guard against overthawing. Begin cleaning and cutting as soon as a knife enters the flesh. Sprinkling fish with salt, sakè, ginger, or ginger juice during thawing stabilizes flavors and improves aromas.

1. *Low-temperature thawing.*   Thaw seafood at low temperatures, preferably in the refrigerator. This inhibits the actions of enzymes and microorganisms. Thaw slow to minimize drip, thus inhibiting alterations in proteins and fats.
2. *Room-temperature thawing.*   Even under these conditions, it is best to thaw in places where the temperature is lower than 24°F.
3. *Thawing in running water.*   Whole fish may be thawed in this fashion. Put the fish in a plastic bag, tightly sealed at the mouth to prevent direct contact, and let the fish stand under running cold water.

Thawing with a microwave oven is undesirable because uneven. If this system must be used, partly thaw with microwaves and complete thawing according to some other method.

Seafoods that freeze well include tuna, mackerel, horse mackerel, turbot, and squid. Those that freeze poorly include cod, crab, and all roes.

Use thawed seafood as soon as possible since its quality will drop quickly even stored in a refrigerator. Much of the seafood on the market has already been frozen once. Freezing it again at home doubles the process and causes serious alterations in proteins and fats. If you do not intend to use your purchase at once, it is probably wiser to buy seafood that is still frozen and has not been thawed for display in the market.

Home Freezing
If the family fisherman has had a big catch, fish may be frozen at home and stored for a month without losing flavor. It is best to remove gills and viscera before freezing. Put the fish in plastic bags. Squeeze out as much air as possible. Since quick freezing is desirable, spread the fish flat on a metal tray. For later reference, write date of freezing on each parcel. Freeze in small batches that can be consumed in one meal.

Fishy Odors on Hands
Fishy smells that resist all washing with soap and water can be an embarrassment. Before you begin working with fish, rub your hands with lemon juice. When your cooking is done, wash them well with soap and water and rub in a little more lemon juice.

Cutting-board Odors
The cutting board is usually wet during work. When you have finsihed with it, wash the board with cold water and a sponge sprinkled with salt. Or you may rub the board with the cut end of a lemon.

Kitchen Odors
To clear the kitchen air of lingering odors, boil a few celery leaves in water. The odor of celery cancels out fish smells. The same effect is achieved by boiling small amounts of lemon or orange peel.

Serve While Hot!
Fish dishes intended to be eaten hot lose flavor and become smelly if allowed to go cold. Have the table and all ingredients ready before you begin final cooking, since most fish dishes can be prepared in short order.

Equipment

Each national cuisine employs distinctive knives. The following 2 are characteristic of Japanese kitchens.

Standard kitchen knife *(Hōchō)*
This kind of knife, which in Japan has a single cutting edge of hard steel forged to a blade of ordinary steel, serves practically all ordinary kitchen purposes. It may be used to cut meat or fish, to julienne slice vegetables, and to peel and slice fruit. It is available in many lengths; perhaps a 7-in blade is most practical for ordinary purposes.

Cleaver *(Deba-bōchō)*
This heavy-duty knife has a pointed edge and a thick blade. It is a good idea to have one for use in cutting and filleting fish.

Cutting board *(Manaita)*
1. *Wooden cutting boards* are easier on knives but breed bacteria if improperly cared for. Always wash and dry the board after use. Occasionally allow it to stand in strong sunlight, which has an antiseptic effect. Wet the board before use to prevent odors and stains from clinging to it.
2. *Plastic cutting boards* are more hygienic. Nonetheless, they too should be disinfected in kitchen bleach from time to time. After their bath in bleach, wash them thoroughly and allow them to dry for half a day.

Colander
Colanders occur in various materials, including plastic, stainless steel, and woven

bamboo. A stainless-steel colander, which will last a long time if washed and dried carefully after each use, is very convenient.

Chopsticks

It is a good idea to have 2 or 3 sets of long, bamboo, kitchen chopsticks on hand. The 2 sticks are joined by a string, which should be cut. In addition to protecting the hands during deep-oil frying, chopsticks serve a number of other useful functions. For instance, a dry chopstick inserted in hot oil gives off fine bubbles that help the cook approximate oil temperature. Or it is possible to judge degree of doneness with relative accuracy by lightly tapping surfaces of fried foods with chopsticks. Of course their use requires a modicum of skill. Until you acquire it, use tongs. Once you have mastered them, however, you will be delighted with the speed and ease with which you can use chopsticks to beat eggs, blend salad oil, turn meat in a frying pan, arrange cooked foods on serving dishes, and so on.

Graters

Both metal and plastic graters are marketed. Metal ones combine two coarsenesses and frequently come equipped with a receptacle for grated ingredients. Some plastic graters are part of a set of slicers and cutters that may be alternately fitted to a container. To grate *daikon* radish, use the finest blades of a cheese grater.

Skewers
Bamboo skewers from 6 to 8 in long are very convenient in judging doneness of various foods and in deveining shrimp.

Scaler
Move the scaler against the scales.

Tweezers
Large metal tweezers are useful in pulling out fish bones.

Tempura equipment
1. *Wok or tempura pan*
   The tempura pan is made of thick metal. The wok is recommended because it permits the frying of tempura in a minimum amount of oil.
2. *Draining pan and rack*
3. *Wire-mesh scoop*
   For removing stray bits of fried batter from oil.

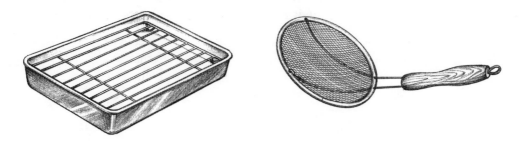

Omega-3 fatty acids: EPA (eicosapentaenoic acid), DHA (docosahexaenoic acid)
Although animal fat is generally recognized to increase blood-cholesterol levels, which plays a role in cardiovascular diseases, the eskimos of Greenland, who eat a great deal of seal meat and fish, are known to have a low rate of arteriosclerosis incidence. Because seals themselves consume large quantities of fish, seal meat

contains a great deal of fat resembling fish fat, which, unlike saturated beef and pork fat, is polyunsaturated.

Among fatty acids, highly unsaturated eicosapentaenoic acid (EPA) is known to reduce bad cholesterol (LDL) while increasing good cholesterol (HDL). Lowering blood-cholesterol levels has the effect of restraining coagulation of blood platelets and thus preventing thrombotic illness. In simpler language, it makes thick, sluggish blood flow smoothly and briskly. Although salmon, halibut, sea snapper, and fish in general all contain it, such fish as sardines, horse mackerel, mackerel, mackerel pike, and yellowtail are especially rich in EPA.

To make full use of EPA, boil or pan fry instead of roasting fish containing it. During roasting, fats drip from the fish, taking EPA with them. To prevent EPA from escaping into the oil, coat fish in breading or batter before frying. Choose the freshest fish possible, since EPA oxidizes easily. Prepare them soon after purchase and eat them as soon as they are cooked. These points are all important from the standpoint of both flavorful eating and good nutrition. Canners usually use very fresh fish, and their products are to be recommended.

Taurin

The sulfur-containing amino acid taurin, present in large amounts in oysters, other shellfish, squid, and shrimp, operates to return high blood pressure to normal levels and to remove cholesterol deposited on blood-vessel walls, thus helping prevent cardiac infarction and arteriosclerosis. It helps control levels of neutral fats, which stimulate hardening of the arteries. Moreover, it has salutary effects on the vision.

In the past, many people avoided oysters, squid, and shrimp because of their high cholesterol content. But, since they contain 8 times as much taurin as cholesterol, these seafoods may be regarded as safe in this connection. A taurin content of 4 times as much as cholesterol content is considered safe, and even twice as much taurin as cholesterol proves effective over protracted periods. Oysters contain 6.5 times as much taurin as cholesterol, and the value for most other shellfish is more than 11. The broths and liquids in which these foods are cooked should be drunk since taurin is water-soluble.

Suggested Menus

Miso Soup with *Wakame* and Tofu (p. 45)
Mixed Tempura (p. 68)
Fruit Salad with Yogurt Dressing
Angel-food Cake

Serve soup and tempura together. The addition of a fritter to the Mixed Tempura makes the meal more luxurious. Hot steamed rice is the suitable starch. When serving tempura, avoid cold desserts.

Manhattan-style Clam Chowder
Oil-baked Halibut (p. 85)
Macaroni Salad with Mayonnaise
A Gelatin Dessert

This is a good dinner menu for busy evenings. The soup and the gelatin dessert may be prepared the day before.

Pumpkin Soup
Broiled Salmon with Sesame and Ginger (p. 84)
Orange Sections and Grapes on Lettuce with Cottage Cheese
Baked Tomatoes
Apple Pie

This is a warming autumn dinner. To prepare the soup, thin canned pumpkin with milk, add butter, and heat. Cut crosses in tops of tomatoes, add a dab of butter, and bake in a medium oven.

Miso Soup with Short-neck Clams (*Asari*) (p. 44)
Bread Fried Salmon with Almonds (p. 70)
Salad of Chopped Tomatoes and Scallions with French Dressing
Mashed Potatoes and Leaf Lettuce
Chocolate Cake

Children Relish this menu. Canned chopped clams facilitate preparation of the soup.

Mushroom, Celery, and Carrot Soup
Japanese-style Griddle Cake (*Okonomiyaki*) (p. 114)

Jako and Rice Salad (p. 32)
Fresh Fruit and Sherbet

Family and friends enjoy cooking and eating *okonomiyaki* together in a relaxed atmosphere. Serve with breads and cooked rice.

Oyster and Spinach Soup (p. 41)
Baked Cod in Radish Sauce (p. 92)
Macédoine of Beets and Potatoes
Banana-nut Muffin

Recommended for cold weather. Use canned beets and boiled potatoes for the macédoine. Dice them and mix with mayonnaise.

Cream-of-corn Soup
Yellowtail *Teriyaki* (p. 63)
Macaroni and Cheese
Artichoke Hearts and Black Olives with Shredded Lemon Peel
Ice Cream and Banana with Chocolate Syrup

Another good menu for busy evenings. Boil macaroni till it still offers some resistance to biting. Boil it with cream, grate cheese into it, and continue heating till cheese melts.

Clam Broth (p. 42)
Cod Paprika (p. 91)
Tossed Salad Garnished with Sliced Almonds
Sherbet with Mixed Fruit

Recommended for luncheon. Let the clams stand in salted water overnight to eject sand. Lightly toast sliced almonds.

Chicken-noodle Soup
Cod and Shrimp Casserole with Potatoes (p. 95)
Buttered Broccoli and Corn
Ice Cream and Banana Topped with Sliced Almonds

Even children who do not like seafood like this menu. Lightly toast sliced almonds.

Minestrone
Salt-baked Horse Mackerel with Watercress (p. 87)
Shrimp and Avocado Salad (p. 29)
Your Favorite Pudding

Minestrone contains enough vegetables to eliminate need for a separate vegetable course.

> Crab and Asparagus Savory Custard (*Chawan-mushi*) (p. 47)
> Salmon Steak in Red-wine Sauce (p. 58)
> Caesar Salad
> Chocolate Mousse

A menu fit for a dinner party. Prepare all ingredients for custard and salmon steak in advance so that the two may be ready at the same time.

> Cream-of-broccoli Soup
> Broiled Swordfish with Dill (p. 85)
> Pineapple and Riccota Cheese on Lettuce
> Cucumber and Carrot Sticks
> Apple Strudel

When you are busy, prepare the fish ahead of time and reheat immediately before serving.

> *Kenchinjiru* (p. 45)
> Tuna Meunière with Cheese (p. 62)
> Tossed Salad with Thousand-island Dressing
> Pork and Beans
> Marble Cake

Kenchinjiru is good made the day before and reheated.

> Cream-of-tomato Soup
> Mackerel in Sour-cream Sauce
> Buttered Asparagus
> Italian Salad
> Upside-down Cake

Substitute other fish fillet for mackerel if you like.

> Chicken-vegetable Soup
> Haddock and Potato Gratin (p. 95)
> A Salad of *Wakame* and Canned Tuna (p. 33)
> Pecan Pie

This menu is popular with children.

New England Clam Chowder
Swordfish Simmered in Tomatoes (p. 98)
Baked Potatoes (frozen)
Green Salad with Thousand-island Dressing
Cheesecake

Without overlapping them, arrange frozen potatoes, cut for French-fries, on a cooking sheet. Sprinkle with vegetable oil and bake in a medium oven till golden brown.

Dishes recommended for pot-luck suppers

Confetti Sushi (p. 103)
Shrimp Rice (p. 106)
Dried *Sakura* Shrimp and *Wakame* Pilaf (p. 108)
Jako and Rice Salad (p. 32)
Orange Roughy and Pasta Salad (p. 27)
Rice with Horse Mackerel (p. 106)
Salmon Rice (p. 105)
Marinated Smelt (p. 23)
Gold-roast Squid (p. 89)

Index